Denver & Rio Grande Western Depots
-Volume Two-
Utah, New Mexico and Colorado

CLIVE CARTER
&
DAVID CARTER

Contents

DATA

	Page
INTRODUCTION	3
MONTE VISTA TO CREEDE	4
TRES PIEDRAS TO SANTA FE	10
LA JARA TO CHAMA	18
MONERO to DURANGO	27
TRIMBLE TO SILVERTON	40
FARMINGTON & OTHER LINES	46
UTAH LINES	52
UTAH BRANCH LINES	91
DENVER & SALT LAKE	125
RIO GRANDE SOUTHERN	148

PHOTOGRAPHS

	Page
	9
	17
	26
	38-39
	45
	51
	87-90
	123-124

ACKNOWLEDGEMENTS	155
ALPHABETICAL INDEX	156
PHOTOGRAPH INDEX	158

INTRODUCTION

This book is the second of two volumes that describe the depots owned by the Denver and Rio Grande Western Railroad. Volume I covers the majority of the buildings in the state of Colorado.

The remainder of the D&RGW Colorado depots and those in Utah, together with New Mexico, are addressed here. A summary of the depots operated by the Rio Grande Southern and Denver & Salt Lake railroads is included,

Depots in Colorado belonging to other railroads (UP, AT&SF, CBQ, C&S and smaller railroads) are summarized in Volume III.

Descriptions of the D&RGW structures, complemented by drawings of them, are presented. Basic information includes the dates of their construction and retirement. Information was collected from several sources. The predominant source was the Interstate Commerce Commission Survey Reports prepared on site by the Commission's Field Engineers in c1920 as part of the Valuation process. The engineers generated a detail description of each structure, usually including a hand drawn plan and cross section(s).

The drawings are reproduced herein. The position of windows or doors in their drawings was not illustrated because such information was not pertinent to the Valuation process. We have also made reference to Valuation update reports prepared by the railroad periodically between 1920 and 1980 for the ICC. Basically, an update was a compilation of the railroad's Authorities For Expenditure for work completed during the reporting period.

Information with respect to structural modifications made to individual structures and their eventual disposal was collected in this way. Drawings of buildings constructed after 1920, when found in company records, were also used.

Other sources consulted included the construction and changes book started in 1890 by the Denver and Rio Grande Railroad Bridges & Buildings Department, and a D&RG 1892 list of structures and their overall dimensions. Sanborn Fire Insurance maps helped to clarify construction dates for several depots built in the 1880's.

Plat maps presented herein depict the location of each depot in relation to the main track; not all secondary tracks are necessarily shown. Nearby water tanks, stockyards and engine houses are noted. The direction of Denver indicated on plats is by rail, not geographic.

The single word "Depot" is used throughout the book to identify a combination passenger and freight structure having facilities for both types of service. The terms "Passenger Depot" and "Freight Depot" are used to identify a building having a specific function.

Where a new depot replaced another, data for both is presented in chronological order. Similarly. passenger buildings are listed before freight for each location. At certain points a simple shelter shed, often a converted freight car body, sufficed for passengers and freight. They are omitted here.

Monte Vista to Creede

Miles from Denver to:

Monte Vista, CO	264.21
Del Norte, CO	278.05
Wagon Wheel Gap, CO	307.32
Creede, CO	315.90

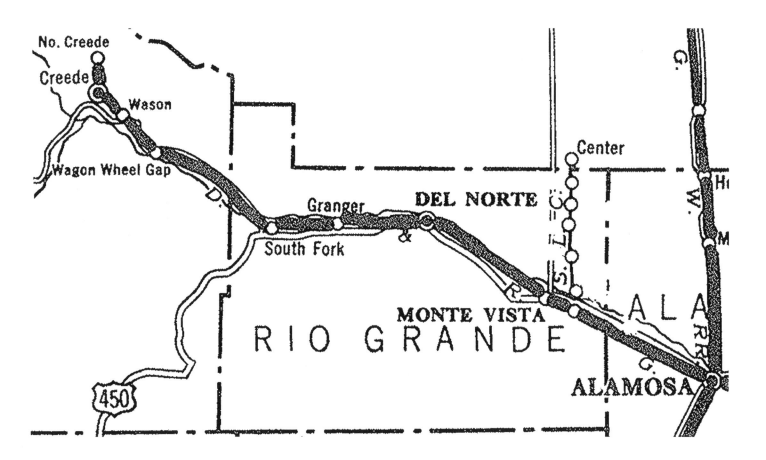

Monte Vista, CO

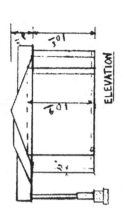

Second Depot-Rear View.

Second Depot-Front View.

Third Depot.

FREIGHT DEPOT

PASSENGER DEPOT   TANK   To Denver →

FIRST DEPOT

Built: 1886.
Construction: One-story frame structure of 16' x 89'.

Converted to freight depot c.1907.
54' portion retired 1937.

SECOND DEPOT

Built:1907.
Construction: One-story brick passenger and baggage depot of 24' x 70'.
Roof: Gable, tile.
Walls: Brick.

Remodeled 1939.
Rebuilt 1947.

THIRD DEPOT

Built: 1947.
Construction: Second depot rebuilt and extended to provide a central portion 25' x 68', with 4' x 16' bays each side. Two wings 19' x 39' (Express and Baggage) and 30' x 48' (Freight).
Walls: Cinder block and stucco.

Partially retired 1978.

Del Norte, CO

FIRST DEPOT

Built: 1881.
Construction: One-story frame structure of 20' x 65'.

Torn down 1910 and replaced by new depot on same site.

SECOND DEPOT

Built: 1911.
Construction: Two-story frame structure of 30' x 32', with one-story 22' x 64' addition.
Roof: Gable, wood shingles.
Walls: Stucco finish with 3' drop siding wainscot.

Retired 1970.

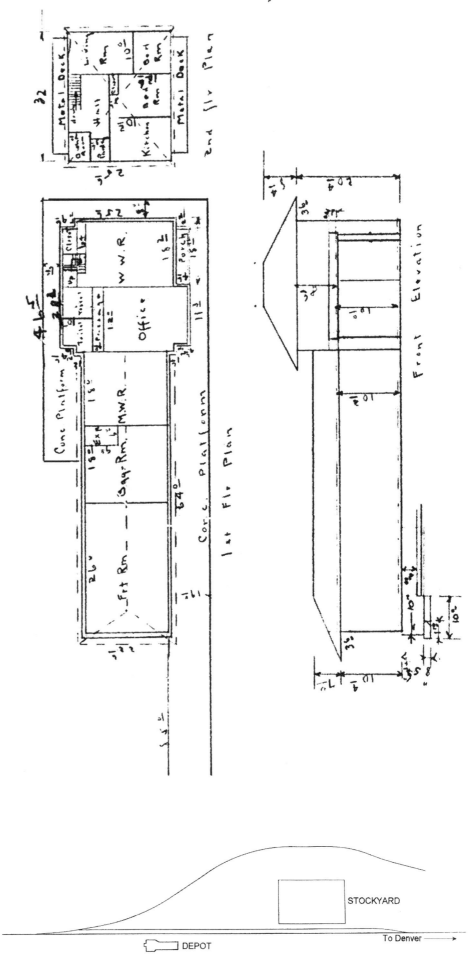

STOCKYARD

DEPOT

To Denver →

Wagon Wheel Gap, CO

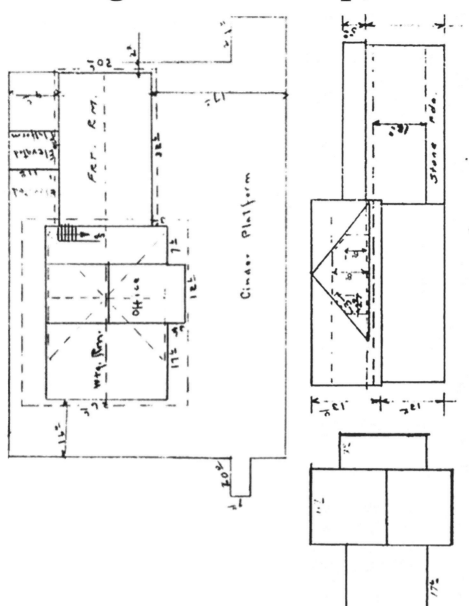

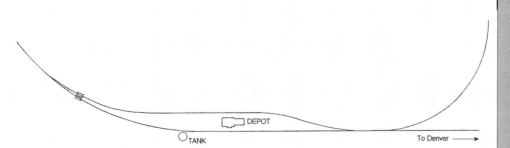

DEPOT

Built: 1883.
Construction: Two-story frame structure of 26' x 37' and one-story portion of 20' x 32'.
Roof: Gable, wood shingles.
Walls: Drop siding.

Retired 1954. Structure still standing at time of writing
ELEVATION: 8449'

DEPOT

Built: 1883.
Construction: Two-story frame structure of 26' x 37' and one-story portion of 20' x 32'.
Roof: Hip, wood shingles.
Walls: Drop siding.

Retired 1954.
Structure still exists at time of writing.

Creede, CO

FIRST DEPOT

Built: 1892.
Construction: One-story frame structure of 24' x 45'. Used as section house from c.1893.

SECOND DEPOT

Built: 1893.
Construction: One-story frame structure of 24' x 97'.
Roof: Gable, wood shingles.
Walls: Board and batten; gable ends wood shingles.

Retired 1961.

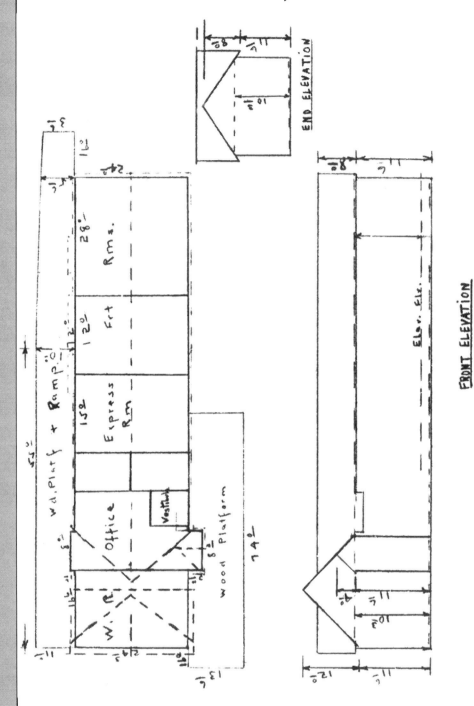

DEPOT

To Denver

8

Photos

Wagon Wheeel Gap

Del Norte

Creede

TRES PIEDRAS TO SANTA FE

Miles from Denver to:

Tres Piedras, NM	310.25
Taos Junction, NM	331.72
Embudo, NM	347.78
Espanola, NM	366.82
Santa Fe, NM	401.10

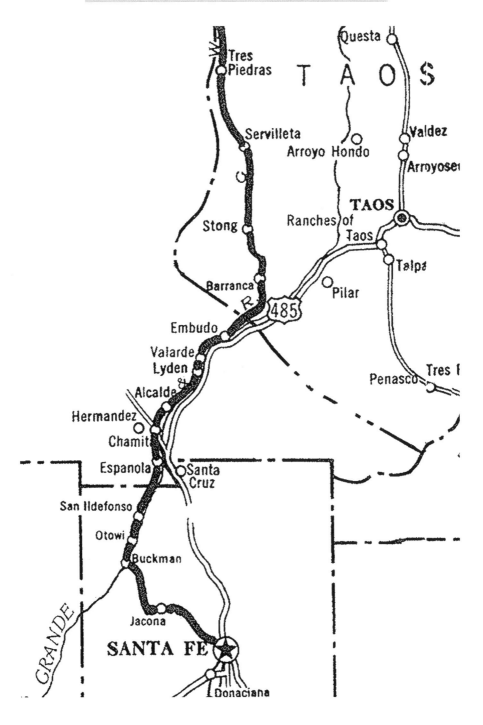

Tres Piedras, NM

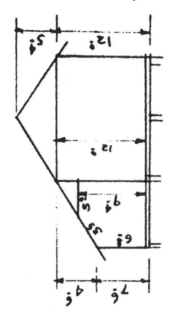

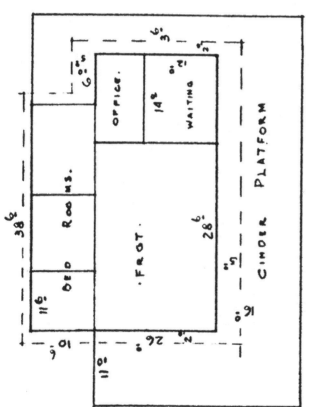

STOCKYARD

To Denver

DEPOT

ELEVATION: 8088'

DEPOT

Built: 1881.
Construction: One-story frame structure of 26' x 28'.
Roof: Gable, wood shingles.
Walls: Lap siding.
By 1920, enlarged to 26' x 45', with a 10' x 17' extension.

Retired 1941.

Taos Junction, NM

FIRST DEPOT

Built: 1881.
Construction: One-story frame 25' x 31'.

Replaced 1915.

SECOND DEPOT

Depot moved from Servilleta in 1915.
Construction: Frame depot of 20' x 96' with two-story 20' x 32' and one-story wing of 20' x 64'.
Roof: Gable, wood shingles.
Walls: Lap siding with 2'6" M&B wainscot.

Retired 1941.

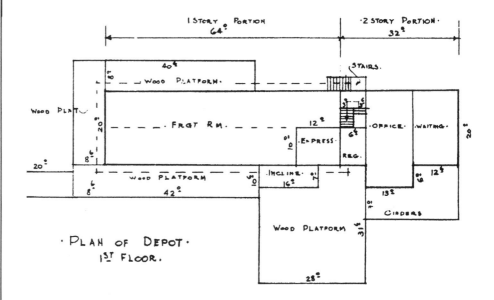

· PLAN OF DEPOT ·
1ST FLOOR.

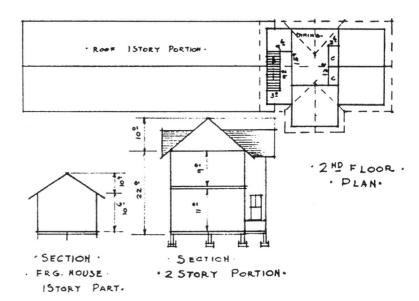

· SECTION ·
· FRG. HOUSE
1STORY PART.

· SECTION ·
· 2 STORY PORTION ·

· 2ND FLOOR ·
· PLAN ·

To Denver

DEPOT

Espanola, NM

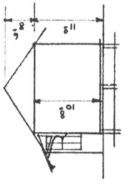

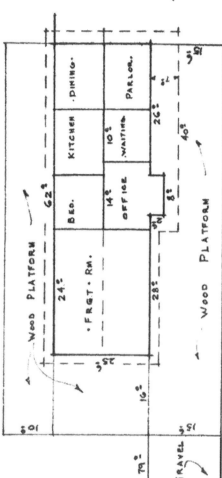

DEPOT

STOCKYARD

To Denver →

Embudo, NM

ELEVATION: 5821'

DEPOT

Built: 1881.
Construction: One-story frame structure of 27' x 33'.
Roof: Gable, wood shingle.
Walls: Boulder dash.

Retired 1941.

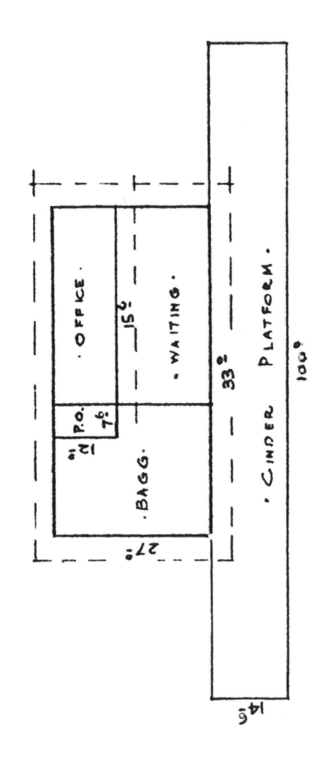

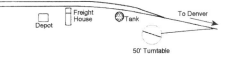

Depot   Freight House   Tank   To Denver

50' Turntable

Santa Fe, NM 1-2

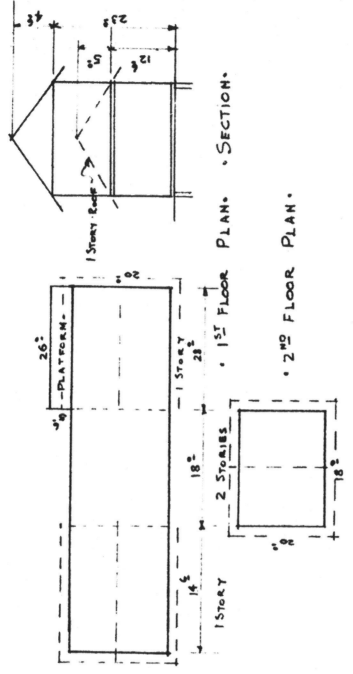

FIRST DEPOT

Built: 1883.
Construction: One and two-story frame structure of 20' x 60'.
Roof: Gable, wood shingles.
Walls: Board and batten.

Retired 1904
(Leased to private party by 1920).

TRANSFER TRACK

WATER COLUMN

FREIGHT DEPOT

PASSENGER DEPOT

To Denver

Garfield Ave.

Montezuma Ave.

Santa Fe, NM 2-2

SECOND DEPOT

Built: 1904.
Construction: One-story brick structure of 24' x 100'.
Roof: Hip, red tiles.
Walls: Brick.

(Jointly owned by D&RGW and New Mexico Central RR.)
Retired 1941.

FREIGHT DEPOT

Approx. 20' x 100'.
Jointly operated.

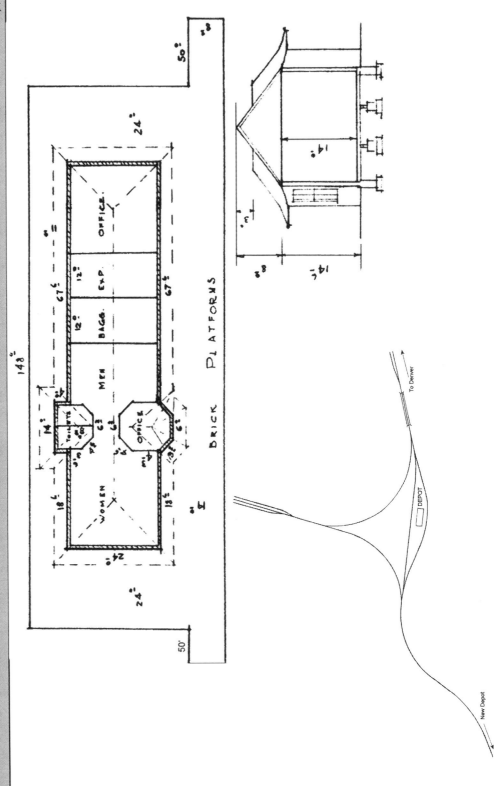

Photos

Taos Junction

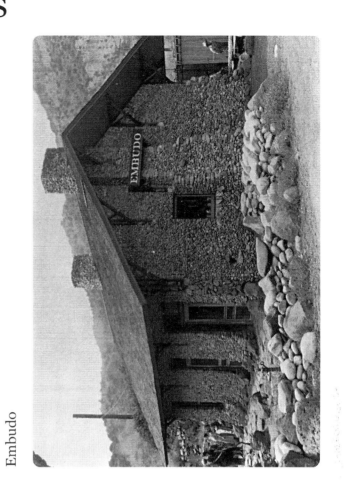

Embudo

Tres Piedras

Esplanola

LA JARA TO CHAMA

Miles from Denver, to:

La Jara, CO	261.36
Romeo, CO	268.47
Antonito, CO	275.52
Sublette, NM	301.26
Osier, CO	313.6
Cumbres, NM	325.8
Chama, NM	339.32

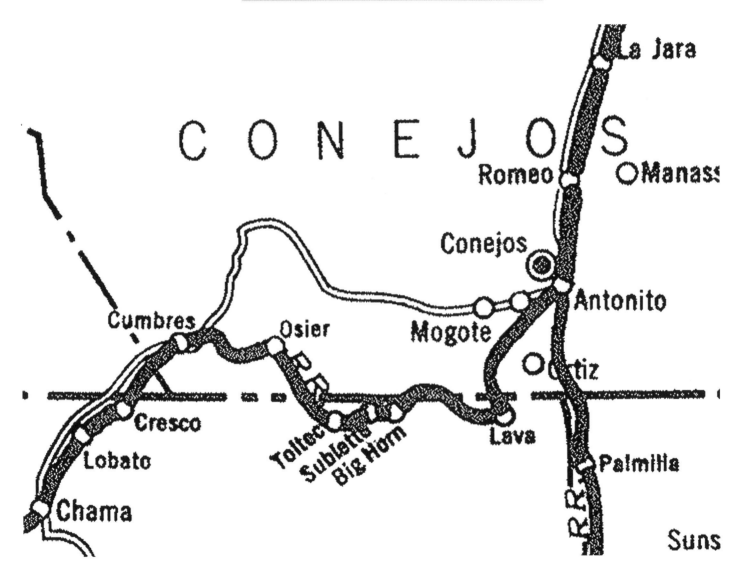

La Jara, CO

ELEVATION: 7609'

FIRST DEPOT

Built: 1886.
Construction: One-story frame structure of 16' x 51'.
Roof: Hip.
Walls: Board and batten with 4' wainscot.

Converted to freight depot c.1911 and retired 1941.

SECOND DEPOT

Built: 1911.
Construction: Two-story frame structure of 25' x 32', with one-story 22' x 44' addition.
Roof: Wood shingles.
Walls: Stucco finish.

Retired 1970.

Romeo, CO

ELEVATION: 7736'

DEPOT

In 1908, the building was moved from Mason.
Construction: One-story frame 24' x 50'.
Roof: Hip, wood shingles.
Walls: Drop siding.

Addition in 1917 of 24' x 20'. Remodelled again in 1937, to provide Agent's living quarters.

Retired 1952.

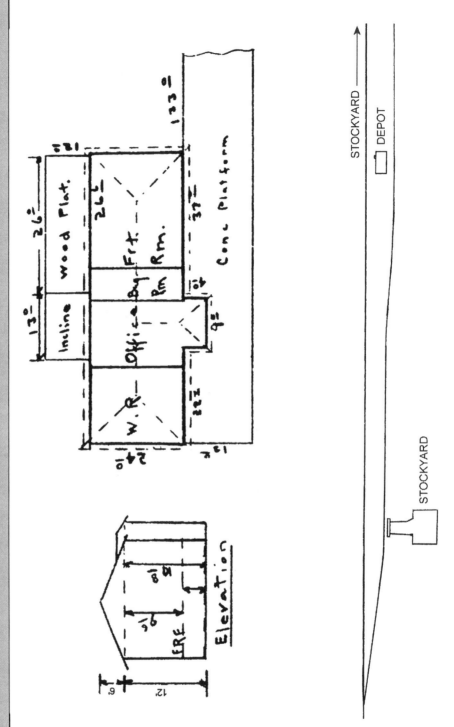

20

Antonito, CO

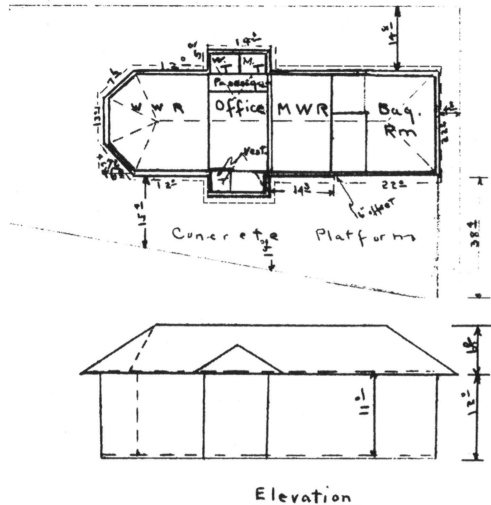

Elevation

PASSENGER DEPOT

Built: 1882.
Construction: One-story stone structure of 22' x 49'.
Addition of 22' x 20' in 1917.

FREIGHT DEPOT

Built: 1880.
Construction: Structure of 21' x 74'.
Attached, 24' x 32' agent's house (later use as section house).
Roof: Hip, wood shingles.
Walls: Stone with stucco finish baggage room.

Freight room and agent's house partially retired in 1944 & 1957.

Completely retired by 1985.

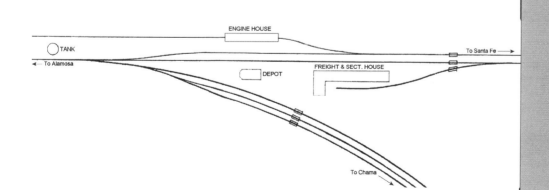

ELEVATION: 9276'

DEPOT

Built: 1882.
Construction: One-story frame structure of 16' x 22'.

Retired by 1920.

Osier, CO

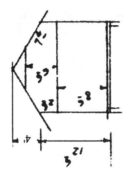

· SECTION·

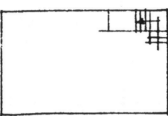

· 2ND FLOOR PLAN·

OFFICE

WAITING

WOOD PLATFORM- 41'

16'

24'

· 1ST FLOOR PLAN·

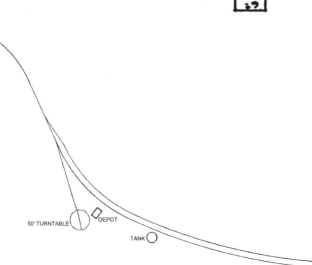

50' TURNTABLE

DEPOT

TANK

To Denver

ELEVATION: 9637'

DEPOT

Built: 1880.
Construction: Two-story frame structure of 16' x 24'.
Roof: Gable, wood shingles.
Walls: Board and batten.

Retired: Not Available.

23

Cumbres, NM

DEPOT

Built: 1882.
Construction: One and one-half story frame structure of 24' x 38'.
Roof: Gable, wood shingles.
Walls: Board and batten walls.

Retired 1953.

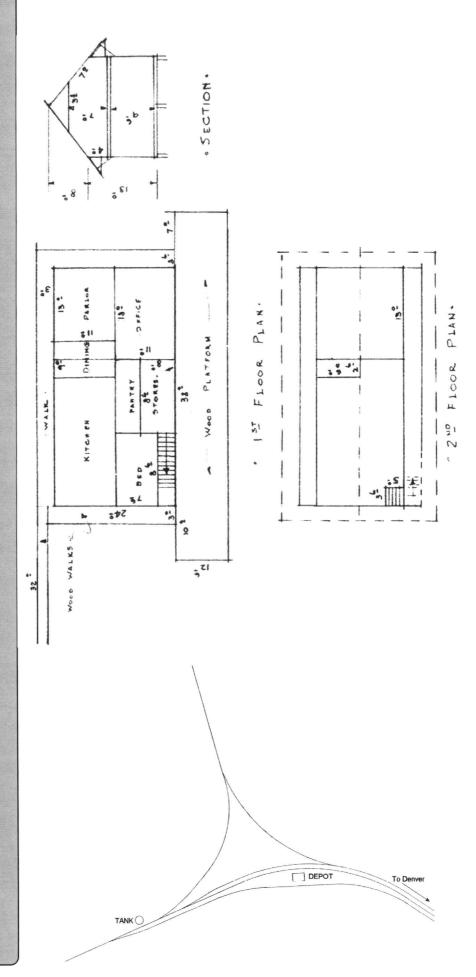

Chama, CO

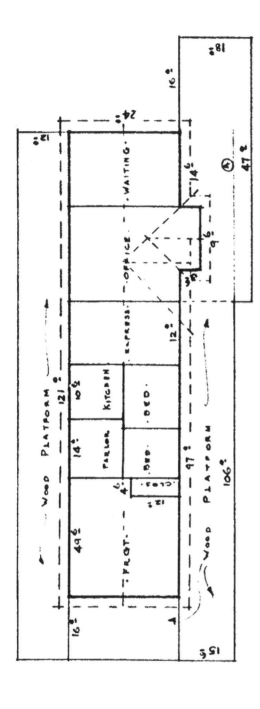

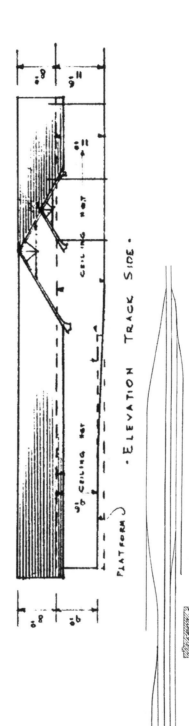

· ELEVATION TRACK SIDE ·

ELEVATION: 7863'

DEPOT

Built: By 1891.
Construction: One-story frame structure of 24' x 121'.
Roof: Gable, wood shingles.
Walls: Board and batten walls.

Currently owned by Cumbres & Toltec Railroad.

Photos

Antonito

Chama

Romeo

Cumbres

MONERO to DURANGO

Miles from Denver to:

Monero, NM	358.67
Amargo, NM	362.09
Lumberton	364.75
Dulce, NM	368.53
Juanita, CO	381.93
Pagosa Jnct, CO	385.56
Arboles, CO	398.83
Allison, CO	406.01
Ignacio, CO	420.94
Durango, CO	446.72

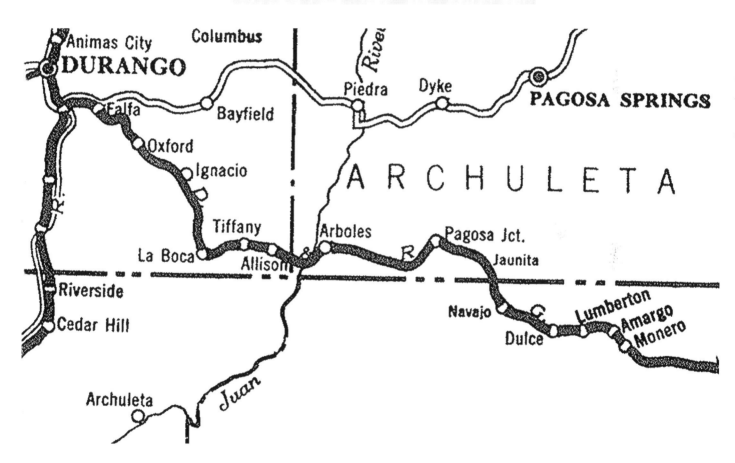

Monero, NM

DEPOT

Built: 1886.
Construction: One-story frame 20' x 44'.
Roof: Gable, wood shingles.
Walls: Board and batten.

Retired 1961.

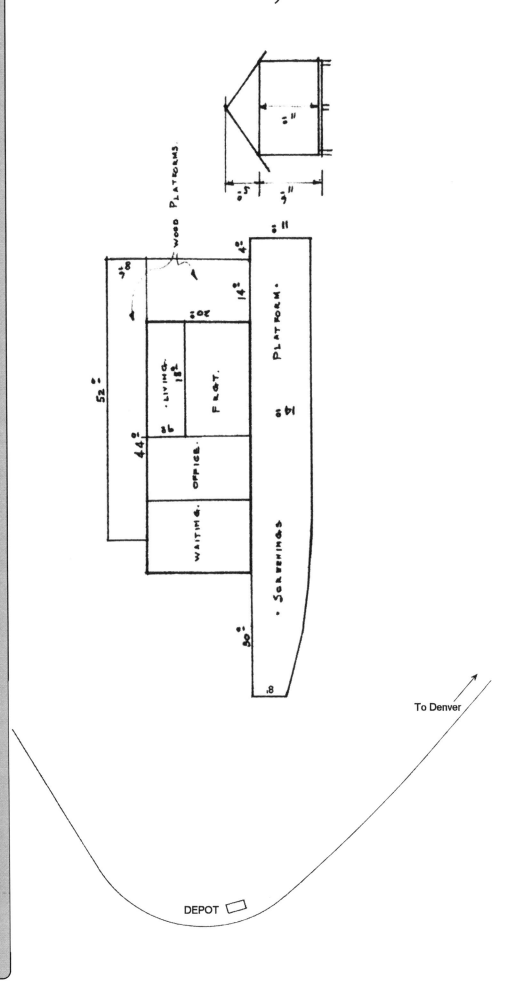

To Denver

DEPOT

Amargo, NM

DEPOT

Built: 1886.
Construction: One-story frame and log structure of 25' x 37', with a 25' x 26' addition.

Moved to Lumberton 1887 (shown as Amargo in 1891 list).

Please see Lumberton for depot plan. (Page 31)

Lumberton, NM

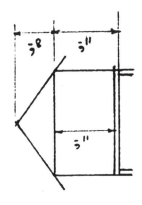

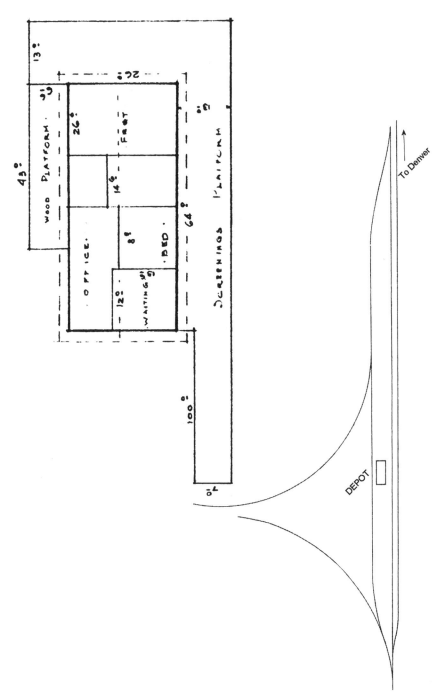

Dulce, NM

To Denver →

DEPOT

Juanita, CO

ELEVATION: 6341'

DEPOT

Built: 1882.
Construction: One-story
frame structure of 25' x 37'.

Moved to Pagosa Jct. c.1900.

ELEVATION: 6341'

Pagosa Junction, CO

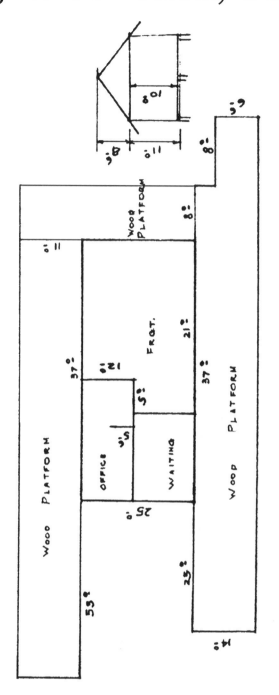

WOOD PLATFORM

FRGT.

OFFICE

WAITING

WOOD PLATFORM

WATER COLUMN

DEPOT

TANK

To Denver

ELEVATION 5562'

DEPOT

Built: By 1893.
Construction: Frame 22' x 90'.
(No details available)

33

Arboles, CO

ELEVATION: 6013'

FIRST PASSENGER DEPOT

Built: 1883
Construction: One-story 16' x 40' frame.
Roof: Gable, wood shingles.
Walls: Lap siding.

Moved to Allison 1922.
Replaced by two car bodies.

SECOND DEPOT

Built: Converted from Section House 1926.
Construction: One-story frame structure of 28' x 44'.

Retired 1964.

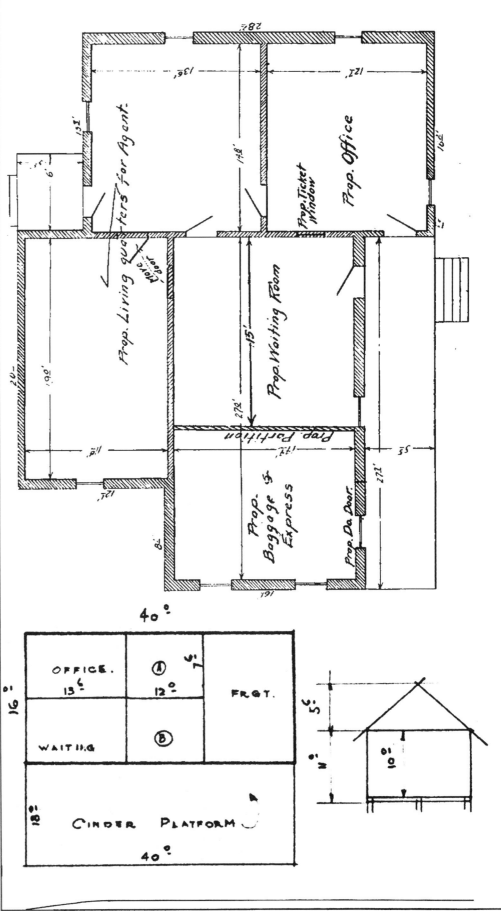

DEPOT   TANK   To Chama →

Allison, CO

To Denver →

☐ DEPOT

DEPOT

Moved: From Arboles 1922.
Replaced passenger and
freight car bodies.
Construction: One-story
frame 16' x 40'.
Roof: Gable, wood shingles.
Walls: Lap siding.

Retired 1968.

Ignacio, CO

FIRST DEPOT

Built: 1881.
Construction: One-story frame structure of 19' x 24'. Enlarged to 19' x 43'. Destroyed by fire October 30, 1917.
Temporarily replaced by two car bodies.

SECOND DEPOT

Built: 1923.
Construction: One-story frame structure of 20' x 119'. (No plan available.)

Retired 1967.

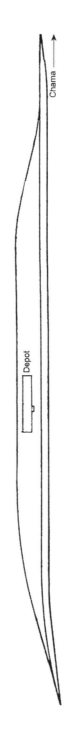

Depot

Chama

Durango, CO

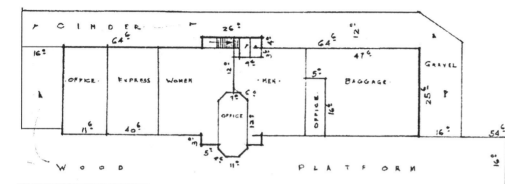

° 1ˢᵀ FLOOR PLAN OF DEPOT °

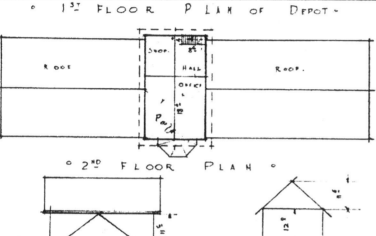

° 2ᴺᴰ FLOOR PLAN °

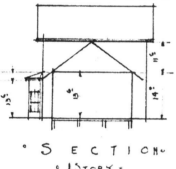

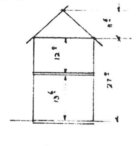

° SECTION °
° 1 STORY °

° SECTION °
° 2 STORY °

ELEVATION: 6520'

DEPOT

Built: 1882.
Construction: Two-story frame structure of 25' x 155'.
Roof: Gable, wood shingles.
Walls: Lap siding with 4'6" M&B wainscot.

Depot still exists at time of writing.

FREIGHT DEPOT

Built: 1881.
Construction: frame structure of 24' x 200'.
Roof: Wood shingles.
Walls: Board and batten.

Retired 1961.

DEPOT

To Rour

Photos

Lumberton

Pagosa Junction

Monero

Dulce

Photos

Allison

Durango

Arboles

Ignacio

TRIMBLE to SILVERTON

Miles from Denver to:

Trimble, CO	455.80
Hermosa, CO	457.72
Rockwood, CO	464.29
Silverton, CO	491.9

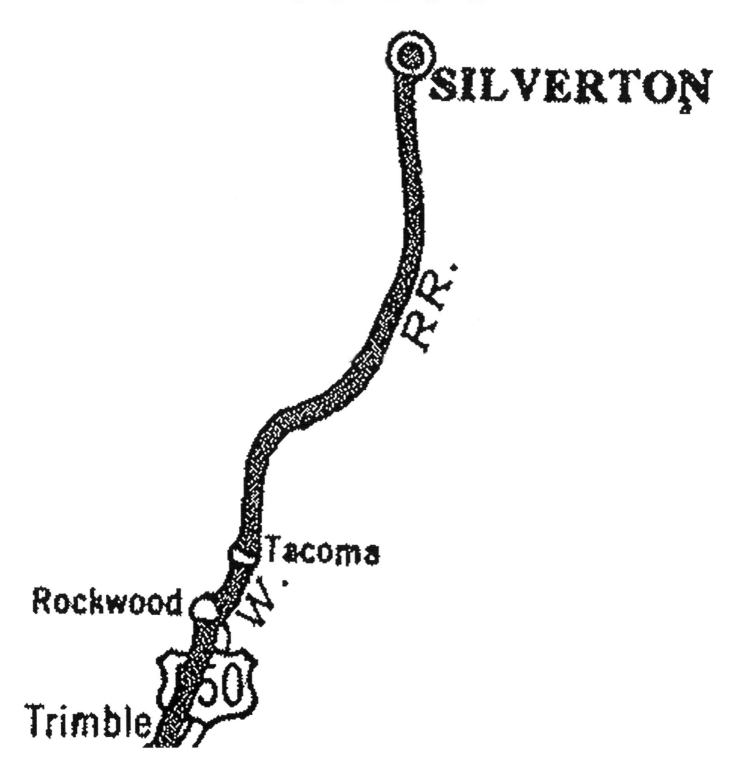

Trimble, CO

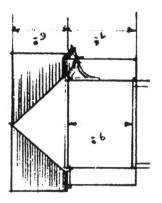

ELEVATION: 6578'

DEPOT

Built: 1883.
Construction: One-story frame structure of 12' x 20', with a 12' x 16' addition.
Roof: Gable, wood shingles.
Walls: Lap siding and wood shingle gable ends.

Retired 1935.

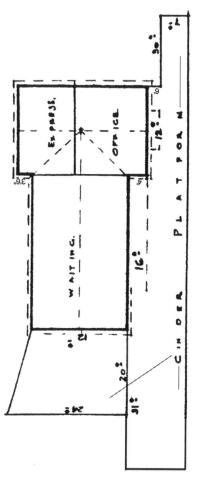

To Denver →

☐ DEPOT

Hermosa, CO

DEPOT

Built: 1883.
Construction: One-story frame structure of 16' x 30'.
Roof: Gable, wood shingles.
Walls: Board and batten.

Retired 1945.

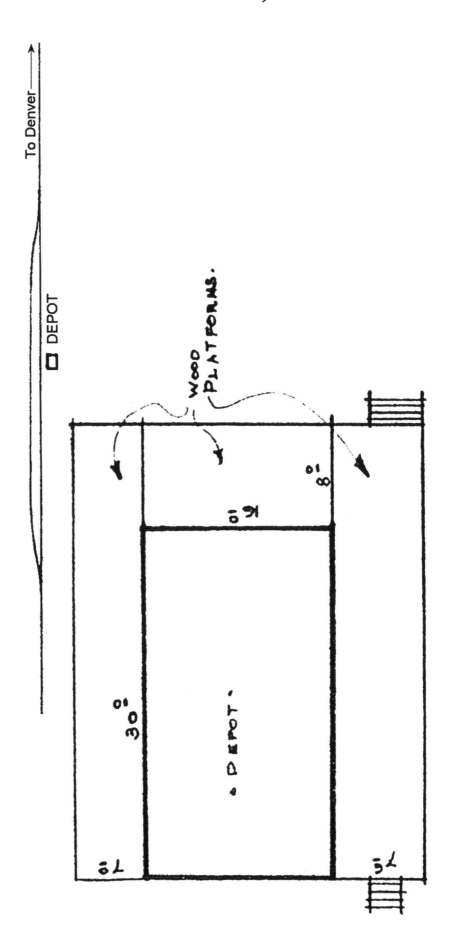

To Denver

DEPOT

WOOD PLATFORMS.

DEPOT

30'

Rockwood, CO

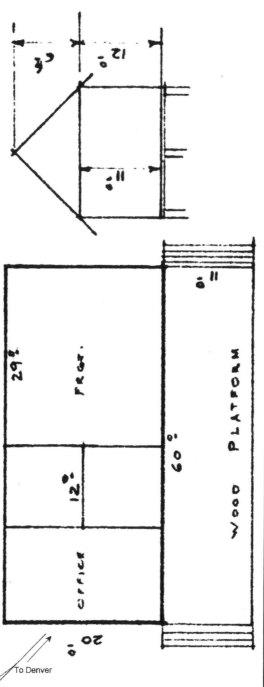

To Denver

DEPOT

STOCKYARD

ELEVATION: 7367'

DEPOT

Built: 1882.
Construction: One-story frame structure of 20' x 60'.
Roof: Gable, wood shingles.
Walls: Board and batten.

Retired and sold 1941.

Silverton, CO

ELEVATION: 9300'

DEPOT

Built: 1882.
Construction: One-story frame structure of 24' x 101'.
Roof: Gable, wood shingles.
Walls: Lap siding with 3' M&B wainscot.

Retired 1969 and donated to San Juan County.

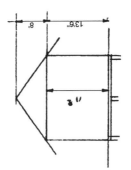

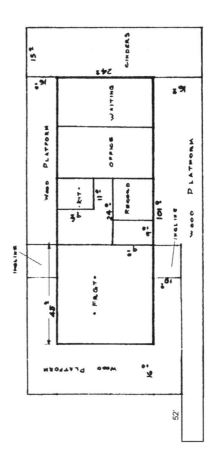

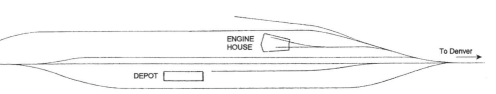

Photos

Silverton

Silverton (Rear) 1977

FARMINGTON, PAGOSA SPRINGS, & LA MADERA LINES

Miles from Denver to:

Aztec, NM	477.0
Farmington, NM	491.4
Pagosa Springs, CO	416.13
La Madera, NM	348.42

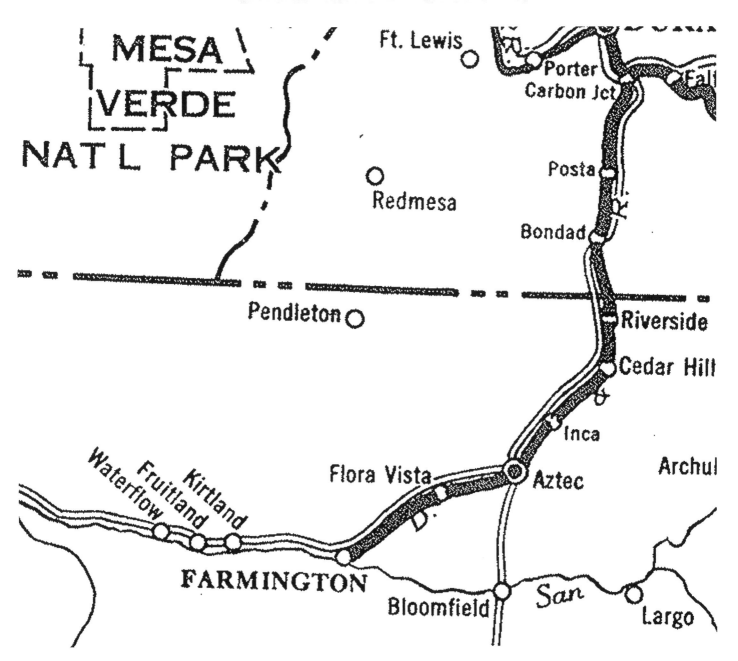

Aztec, NM

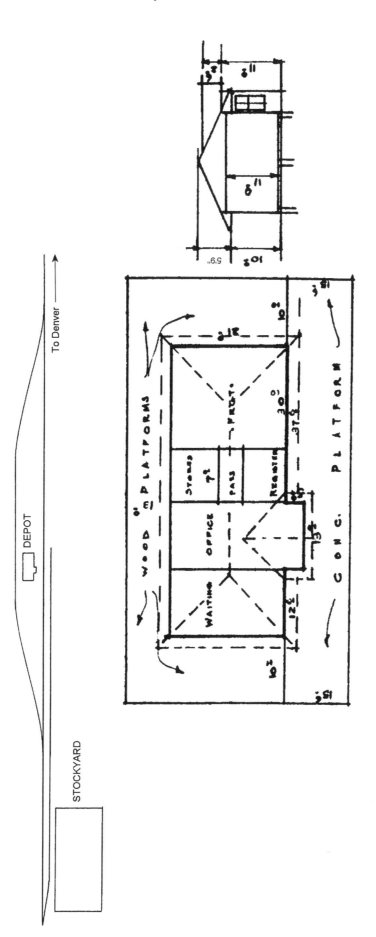

DEPOT

Built: 1905.
Construction: One-story frame structure. Original size unknown.
Roof: Hip, Composition 2.
Wall: Drop siding with 3'4" M&B wainscot.

Burned on November 9, 1914.
Rebuilt in 1915 to 21' x 63'.
Retired c1969.

Farmington, NM

ELEVATION: 5305'

DEPOT

Built: 1906.
Construction: One-story frame structure of 20' x 73'.
Roof: Gable, wood shingles.
Walls: Drop siding with 1'6" M&B around freight room and 4'6" M&B wainscot around remainder of structure.

Demolished by explosion 1963.
Replaced by a metal tool house from Gato.

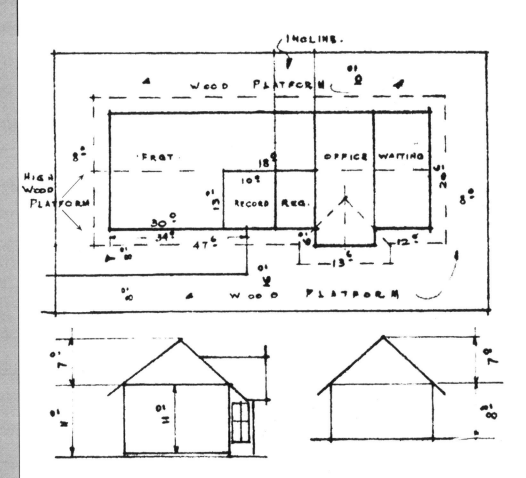

• SECTION OFFICE, WAITING •   • SECTION •
  & PORTION FRGT RM.   • REM. FRGT. RM•

DEPOT ☐   ○ TANK   To Denver →

Pagosa Springs, CO

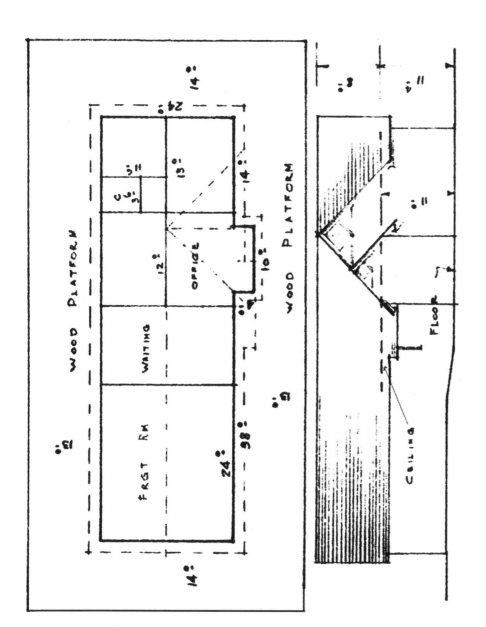

WOOD PLATFORM

WOOD PLATFORM

FRGT RM

WAITING

OFFICE

ELEVATION OF DEPOT.

CEILING

FLOOR

ELEVATION: 7108'

DEPOT

Built: 1935
Construction: One-story frame structure of 24' x 62'.
Roof: Gable, wood shingles.
Walls: Lap siding.

49

La Madera(Mill), NM

ELEVATION: 6750'

<u>DEPOT</u>

Built: 1918.
Construction: One-story
frame structure of 14' x 48'.
Consisted of 14' x 24'
passenger room and 14' x 24'
freight room.

(No floor plan available.)

Retired 1932

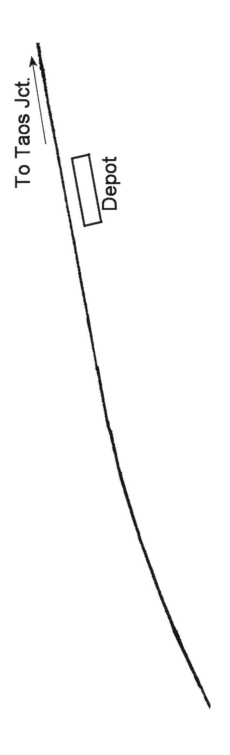

To Taos Jct.

Depot

Photos

Farmington

Aztec (rear)

UTAH LINES

Miles from Denver to:

Fruita, CO	460.5	Mill Fork, UT	669.8
Loma, CO	465.6	Thistle, UT	680.9
Mack, CO	468.9	Mapleton, UT	691.3
Ruby, CO	473.4	Springville, UT	695.8
Westwater, UT	488.4	Provo, UT	701.2
Cisco, UT	504.4	Geneva, UT	710.0
Thompson, UT	528.1	American Fork, UT	713.7
Green River, UT	555.2	Lehi, UT	717.0
Woodside, UT	580.6	Riverton, UT	728.6
Mounds, UT	603.2	Midvale, UT	734.5
Price, UT	619.1	Murray Depot, UT	738.4
Helper, UT	626.5	Salt Lake City, UT	745.1
Castle Gate, UT	630.3	Woods Cross, UT	753.6
Kyune, UT	639.3	Kaysville, UT	764.4
Colton, UT	644.5	Layton, UT	767.2
Soldier Summit, UT	651.4	Clearfield, UT	772.0
Giluly, UT	661.0	Ogden, UT	782.0

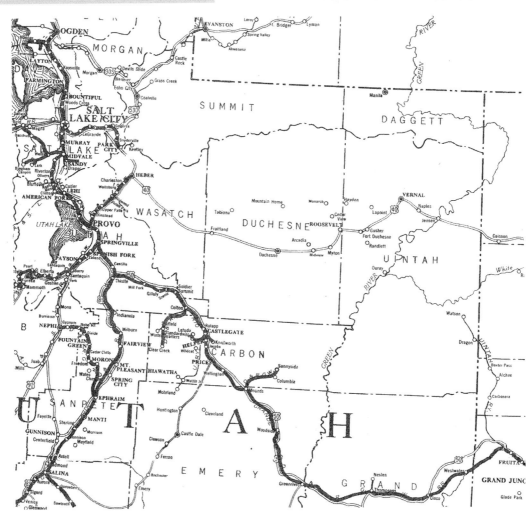

Fruita, CO

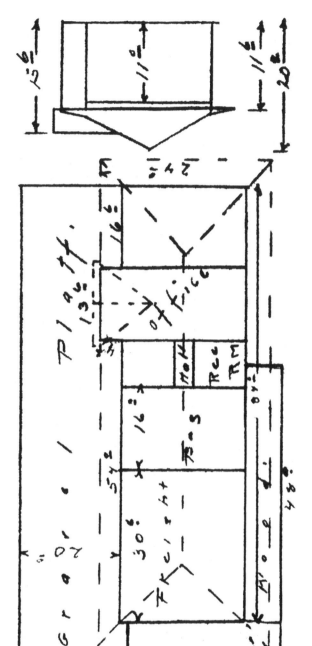

To Denver

STOCKYARD

TANK

DEPOT

ELEVATION: 4510'

FIRST DEPOT

Built: 1911.
Construction: One-story frame structure of 24' x 62', with a 4' x 11' addition.

Burned down on July 3 1913.

SECOND DEPOT

Built: 1914.
Construction: One-story frame structure of 24' x 82'.
Roof: Hip, wood shingles.
Walls: Stucco with 3'7" diagonal pattern wainscot.

Retired 1973.

Loma, CO

DEPOT

Built: 1909.
Construction: One-story
frame structure of 22' x 62'.
Roof: Hip, wood shingles.
Walls: Drop siding.

Retired 1942.

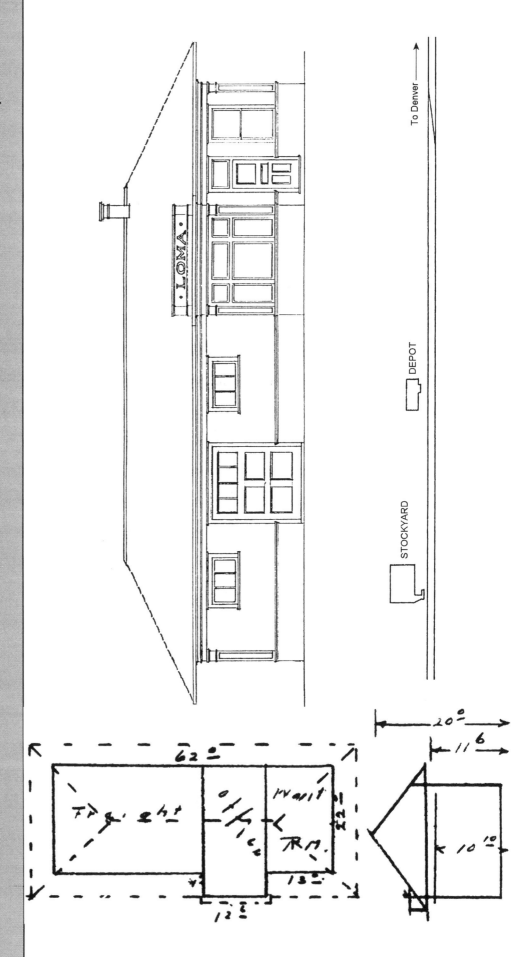

Mack, CO

ELEVATION: 4540'

DEPOT

Built: 1904.
Construction: One-story frame structure of 20' x 71'.
Roof: Hip, wood shingles.
Walls: Drop siding with 3' beaded wainscot.

Jointly owned with Utah Ry. from 1939.

Retired 1954.

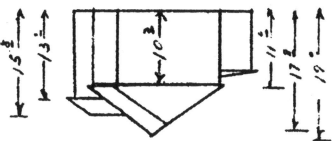

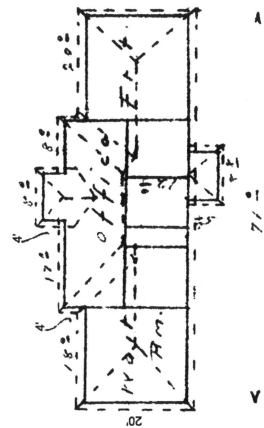

UINTAH RY.

DEPOT

To Denver

To Ogden

Ruby, CO

DEPOT

Built: 1891.
Construction: One-story frame structure of 16' x 24' and 16' x 24' with 16' x 21' rear addition as office and dwelling.
Roof: Gable, wood shingles.
Walls: Board & batten.

Converted to section house by 1920.

Retired c1958.

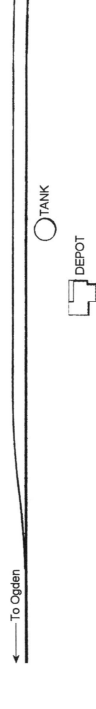

TANK

DEPOT

To Ogden

Westwater, UT

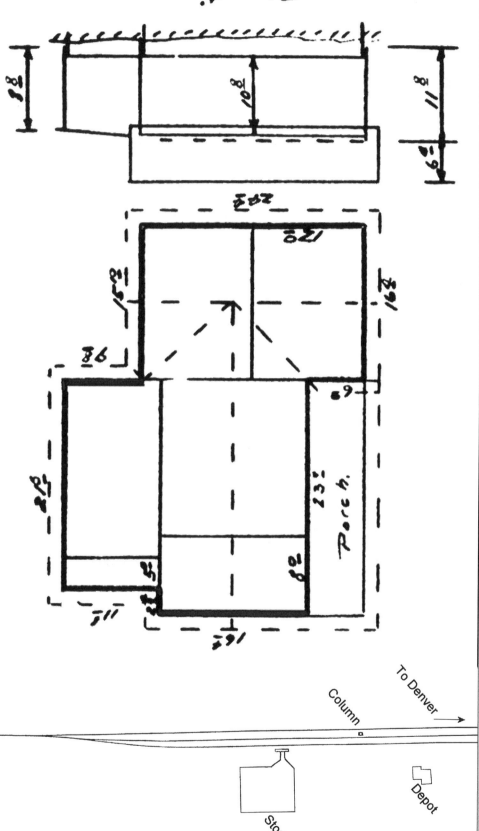

Elevation

18'
10'8"
11'8"
6'3"

24'3"
12'0"
16'4"
8'6"
21'
9'
13'
Porch
9'
11'
16'4"

Column
To Denver
Stock Yard
Depot

ELEVATION: 4316'

DEPOT

Built: 1891 (as section house)
Construction: One-story
frame structure of 16' x 24',
with additions of 16' x 24' and
12' x 21'.
Roof: Gable, wood shingles.
Walls: Board and batten.
Modified to a depot by 1920.

Retired 1953.

Cisco, UT

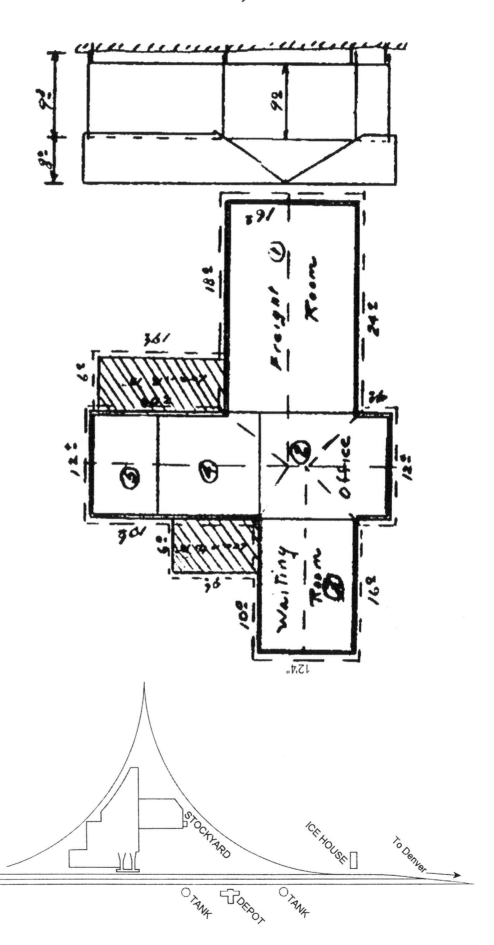

ELEVATION: 4075'

DEPOT

Built: 1890.
Construction: One-story frame structure of 12' x 16', with a 12' x 37' addition.
Roof: Gable, wood shingles.
Walls: Room 1 board & batten on one side and end, lap siding opposite side; Rooms 2 & 3 lap siding; Rooms 4 & 5 drop siding.

Addition of 16' x 24' in 1895.

Retired 1965.

Thompson, UT

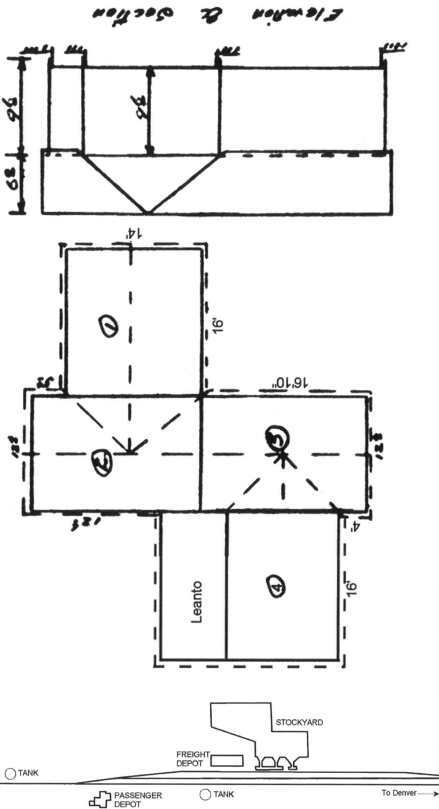

Elevation & Section

Leanto

STOCKYARD

FREIGHT
DEPOT

TANK

PASSENGER
DEPOT

TANK

To Denver →

FIRST DEPOT

Built: 1883.
Construction: One-story frame structure of 12' x 36', with two additions of 14' x 16'.

Roof: Gable, wood shingles.
Walls: Lap siding except room with 1 drop siding.

Retired 1946.

SECOND DEPOT

Built: 1945.
Construction: Frame structure of 28' x 72', with a 4' x 12' bay.
Walls: Concrete.

Survived until at least 1986.

FREIGHT DEPOT

Built: 1889.
Construction: Frame structure of 16' x 54'.
Roof: Wood shingles.
Walls: Board and batten.

Enlarged in 1913 to 24' x 78'.
Retired 1972.

Green River, UT

ELEVATION: 4075'

FIRST DEPOT

Built: c1882.
Construction: One and a half-story frame passenger structure with one-story freight structure attached. No dimensions available.

Retired c1908.

SECOND DEPOT

Built: 1908.
Construction: One-story frame structure of 24' x 112', with a 4' x 16' addition.
Roof: Hip, wood shingles.
Walls: Lap siding.

Retired 1944.

THIRD DEPOT

Built: 1944.
Construction: One-story brick structure of 26' x 70'.
Wall: Brick.
Roof: Flat roof.

No drawing available.

As of writing, the depot still exists.

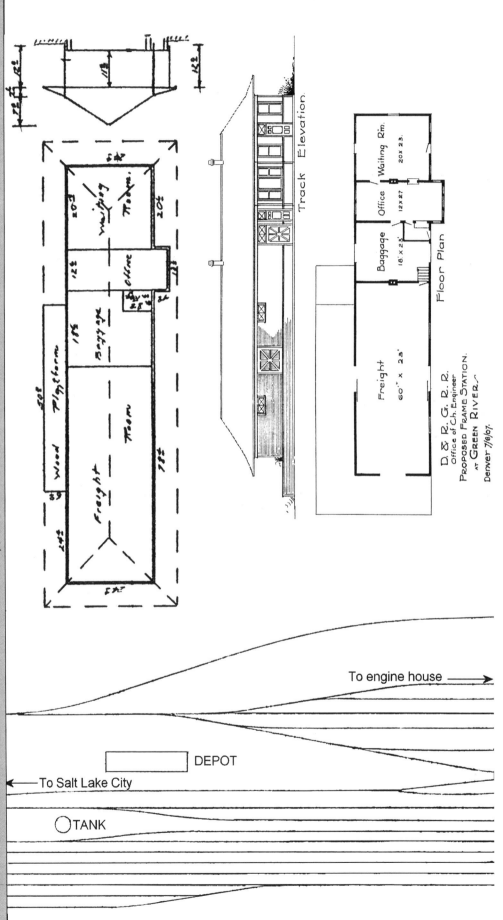

To engine house →

DEPOT

← To Salt Lake City

TANK

Woodside, UT

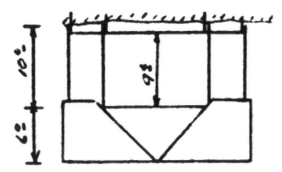

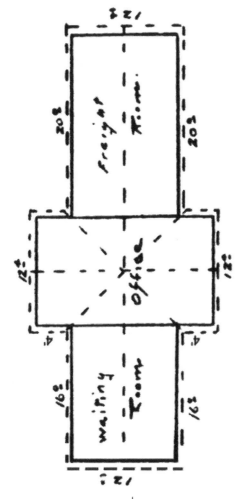

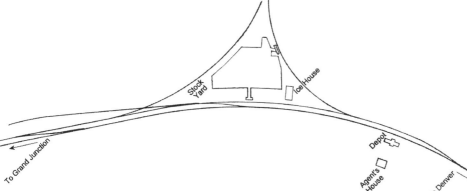

DEPOT

61

Built: 1880.
Construction: One-story frame structure of 12' x 20', with additions of 12' x 20' and 12' x 16'.
Roof: Gable, wood shingles.
Walls: Drop siding except freight room had board and batten on one side and wood shingle gable.

Retired 1944.

Mounds, UT

DEPOT

Built: 1899.
Construction: One-story
frame structure of 26' x 69'.
Roof: Gable, wood shingles.
Walls: Lap siding with 3'6"
beaded wainscot on Part A
and drop siding with 3'6"
beaded wainscot on Part B.

Retired 1964.

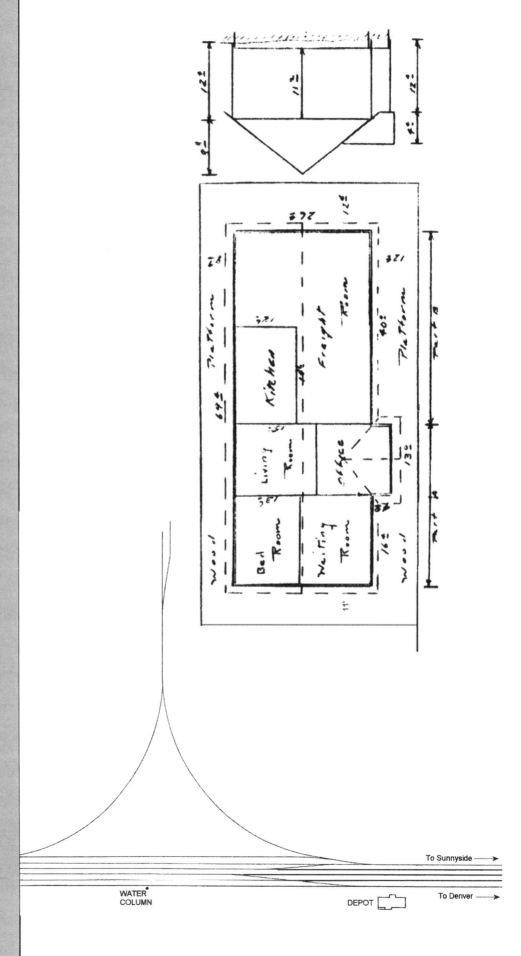

WATER
COLUMN

To Sunnyside →

DEPOT

To Denver →

Price, UT

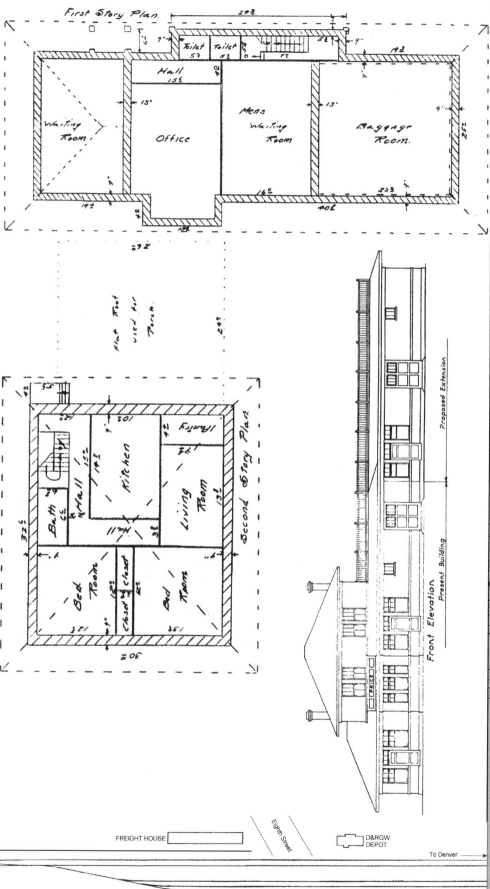

First Story Plan.

Waiting Room

Office

Hall

Mens Waiting Room

Baggage Room.

Toilet
Toilet

Second Story Plan

Kitchen

Pantry

Living Room

Bath

Hall

Bed Room

Closet

Bed Room

Front Elevation
Present Building

Proposed Extension

FREIGHT HOUSE

Eighth Street

D&RGW DEPOT

To Denver

SOUTHERN UTAH RR DEPOT

ELEVATION: 5541'

FIRST DEPOT

Built: 1883.
Construction: One story frame structure of 18' x 49', with a 5' x 14' addition.
Destroyed by fire c1911.

SECOND DEPOT

Built: 1911.
Construction: Two-story brick passenger and baggage depot having a head house of 31' x 32'8". With one-story additions of 16'6" x 25' (west wing) and 24' x 25' (east wing).
Roof: Pyramid and hip, red tile.
Walls: Brick.

East wing extended by 50' in 1928.
Retired 1978.

FREIGHT DEPOT

Built: 1883
Construction: One-story frame structure of 30' x 111'.
Roof: Wood shingles.
Walls: Board & batten.

Extended 1904 to 30' x 210'.
Retired 1978.

Helper, UT

FIRST DEPOT

Built 1892.
Construction: Two-story frame 23' x 66' passenger and baggage depot, with 12' x 20' addition.
Roof: Gable, wood shingles; gable ends with fancy curved shingles.
Walls: Drop siding with 3' beaded wainscot.

Replaced 1946.

SECOND DEPOT

Built: 1946.
Construction: One-story structure of 41' x 123'.
Walls: Cinder block and brick.

(No drawing available.)
At time of writing, depot stil exists.

FREIGHT DEPOT

Built: 1913.
Construction: One story structure of 24' x 76'.
Roof: Corrugated iron.
Walls:. Corrugated iron with 4' wainscot.

Retired 1958.

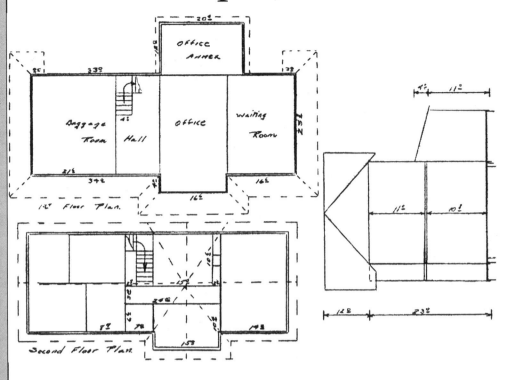

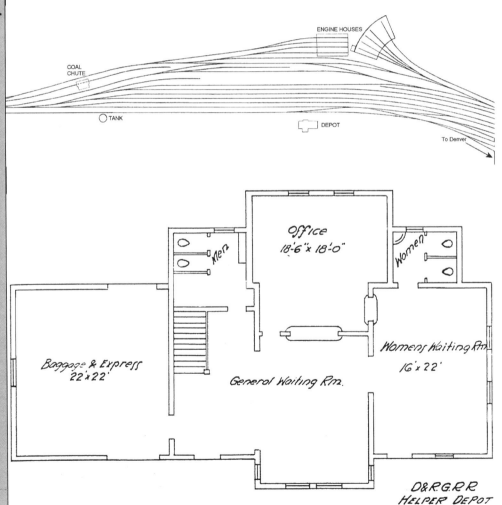

Castle Gate, UT

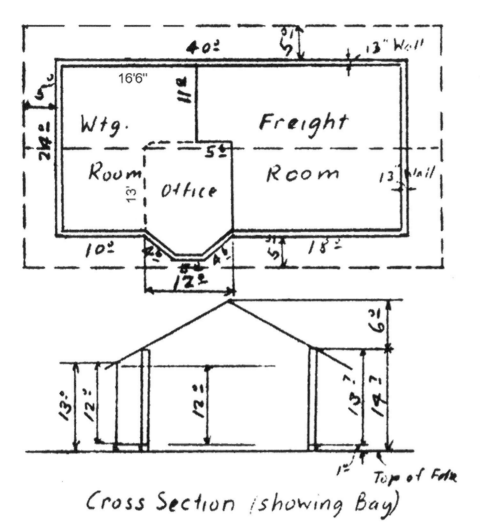

Cross Section (showing Bay)

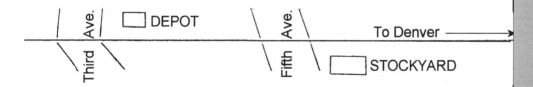

Third Ave. ☐ DEPOT   Fifth Ave.   To Denver →

☐ STOCKYARD

ELEVATION: 6105'

DEPOT   65

Built: 1892.
Construction: One-story
frame structure of 20' x 60',
with two additions of 4' x 17'.

Replaced with two car bodies
by 1920s.

Kyune, UT

DEPOT

Built: Unlisted.
Construction: One-story
frame structure of 24' x 26'.
Roof: Gable, composition
No.2.
Walls: Board and batten.

Changed to operator's house
1950.
Retired 1964.

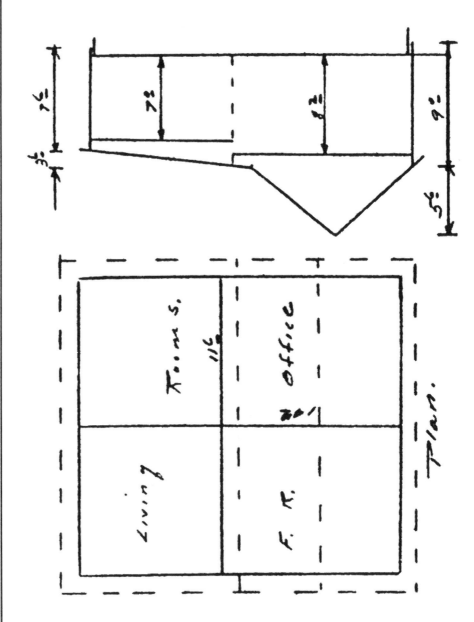

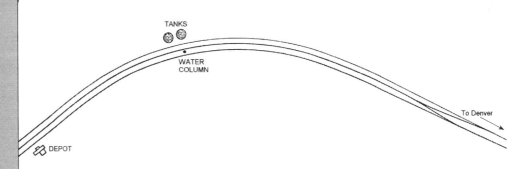

66

Colton, UT

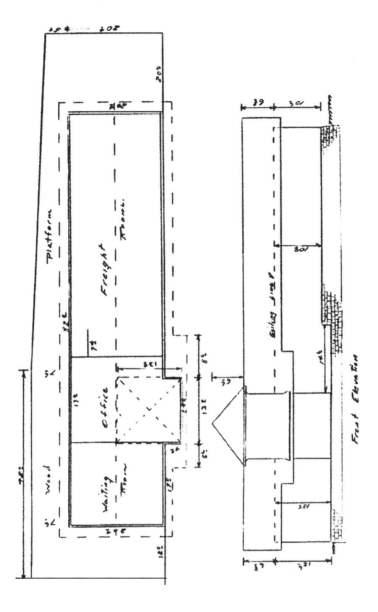

ELEVATION: 7170'

DEPOT

Built: 1892.
Construction: One-story frame structure of 20' x 82', with a 5' x 13' addition.
Roof: Gable, wood shingles.
Walls: Drop siding with 4'6" beaded wainscot; tower wood shingles.

Retired 1947.

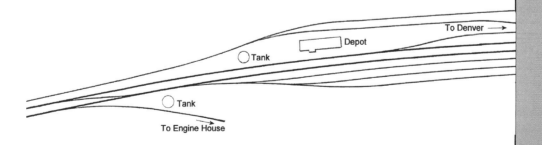

To Denver →

Depot

Tank

Tank

To Engine House →

Soldier Summit, UT

ELEVATION: 7465'

FIRST DEPOT

Two-story frame structure approx. 25' x 40', no details available.

Retired c1919.

SECOND DEPOT

Built: 1918-19.
Construction: Two-story frame structure of 36' x 100', no details available.

Retired 1951.

THIRD DEPOT

Built: 1951.
Construction: Brick structure of 21' x 25'
Walls: Brick.
Roof: Asphalt shingles.

Removed 1988.

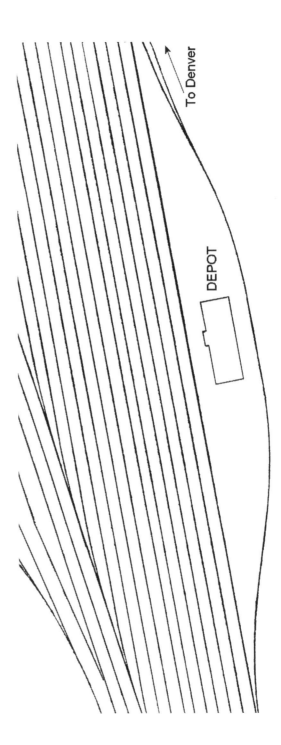

To Denver

DEPOT

Giluly, UT

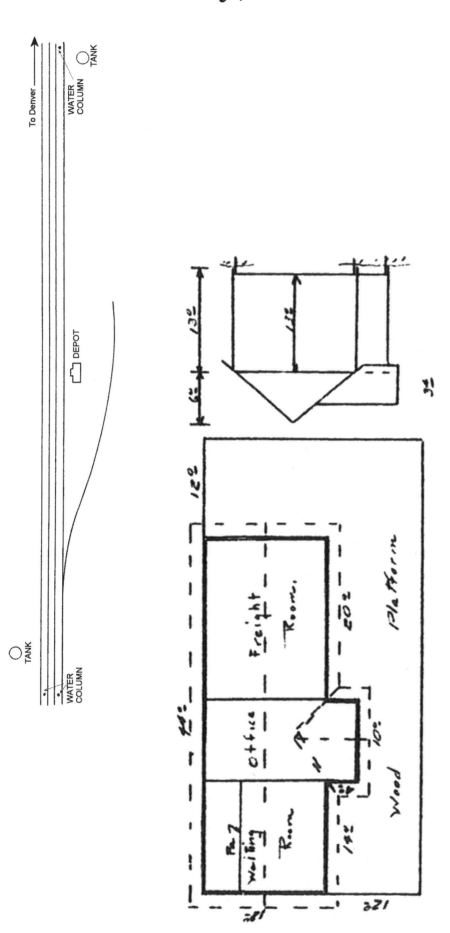

ELEVATION: 5805'

DEPOT

Built: 1901.
Construction: Frame
Telegraph office and dwelling structure of 25' x 30', with additions of 4' x 13' and 8' x 14'.
Roof: Gable, wood shingles.
Walls: Drop siding.

Combination depot and section house by 1920. Converted to section house 1948.

Retired 1961.

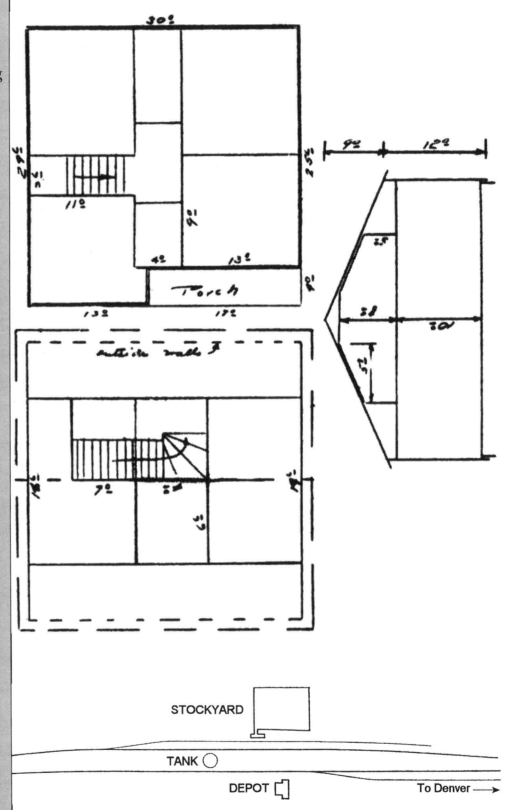

STOCKYARD

TANK ◯

DEPOT

To Denver →

Thistle, UT

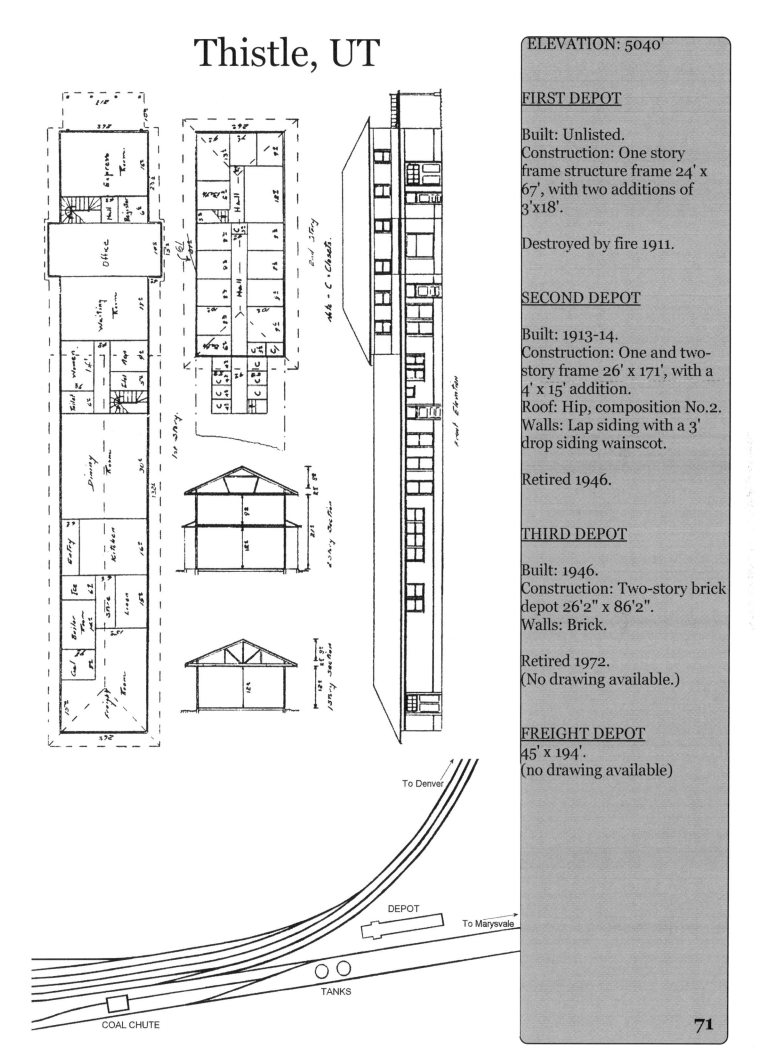

ELEVATION: 5040'

FIRST DEPOT

Built: Unlisted.
Construction: One story frame structure frame 24' x 67', with two additions of 3'x18'.

Destroyed by fire 1911.

SECOND DEPOT

Built: 1913-14.
Construction: One and two-story frame 26' x 171', with a 4' x 15' addition.
Roof: Hip, composition No.2.
Walls: Lap siding with a 3' drop siding wainscot.

Retired 1946.

THIRD DEPOT

Built: 1946.
Construction: Two-story brick depot 26'2" x 86'2".
Walls: Brick.

Retired 1972.
(No drawing available.)

FREIGHT DEPOT
45' x 194'.
(no drawing available)

To Denver

DEPOT

To Marysvale

TANKS

COAL CHUTE

Mapleton, UT

ELEVATION: 4724'

COMBINATION DEPOT AND SECTION HOUSE

Built: 1882.
Construction: One-story frame 18' x 34' (depot) and 25' x 28' (section house).
Roof: Gable, wood shingles.
Walls: Rooms 1, 2 and 3 drop siding, with 4' beaded wainscot; Rooms 4, 5, 6 and 7, board and batten.

Section house only by 1920.

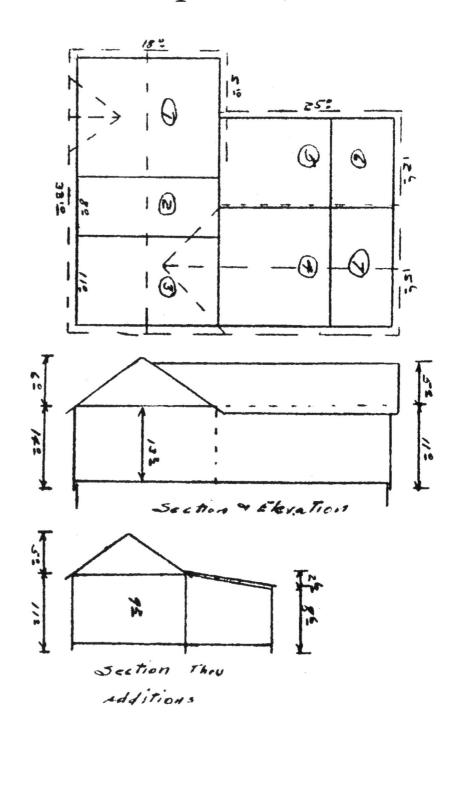

Section & Elevation

Section Thru additions

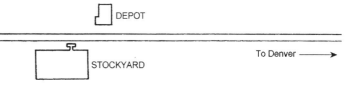

DEPOT

STOCKYARD

To Denver ⟶

Springville, UT

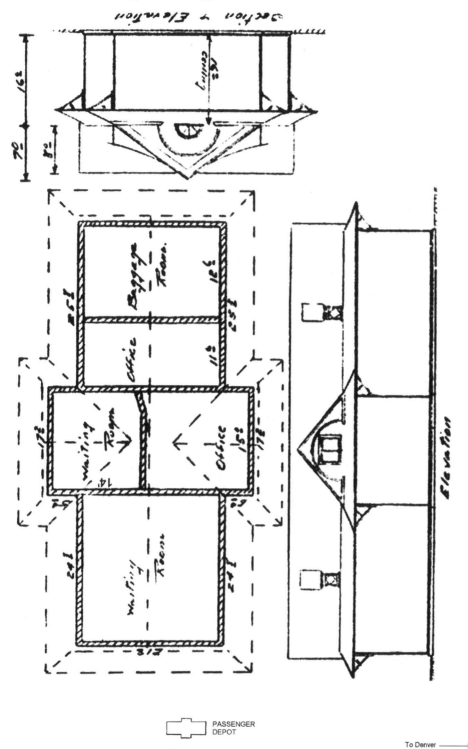

PASSENGER
DEPOT

FREIGHT
DEPOT

TANK

To Denver

WYE

ELEVATION: 4555'

PASSENGER AND BAGGAGE DEPOT

Built: 1889.
Construction: One-story brick structure of 21' x 67', with two additions of 5' x 17'.
Roof: Gable, wood shingles.
Walls: Brick.

Retired 1964.

FRAME DEPOT

Built: 1891.
Construction: Frame structure of 24' x 62'.
Roof: Wood shingle.
Walls: V-Joint with 4' beaded wainscot.

Retired 1947.

ELEVATION 4517'

FIRST DEPOT

Built: 1883.
Construction: One-story
frame structure of 26' x 88'.

Converted to freight depot
c1911.
Retired 1945.

SECOND DEPOT

Built: 1911.
Construction: One-story brick
structure of 30' x 195'.
Roof: Various styles, red tiles.
Walls: Brick.

Enlarged 1945.
Retired 1986.
As of time of writing,
structure still exists

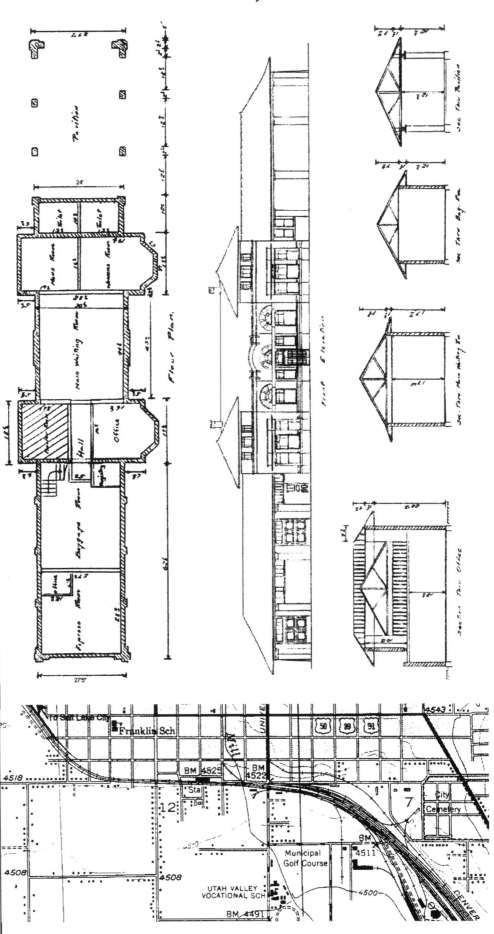

Geneva, UT

To Provo →

☐ Depot

ELEVATION: 4502'

DEPOT

Construction: Shelter shed structure of 7' x 8'.

Replaced by 16'6" x 20'6" depot from Woods Cross in 1942.

ELEVATION: 4563'

FIRST DEPOT

Built: 1893.
Construction: One-story frame structure of 20' x 47'.
Roof: Gable, wood shingles.
Walls: Drop siding with 3' beaded wainscot.

Retired 1954

SECOND DEPOT

Built: 1954.
Construction: One-story lava block structure of 18' x 18'.
Roof: Gable.
Walls: Lava block.

Retired 1986.
(Plan not available.)

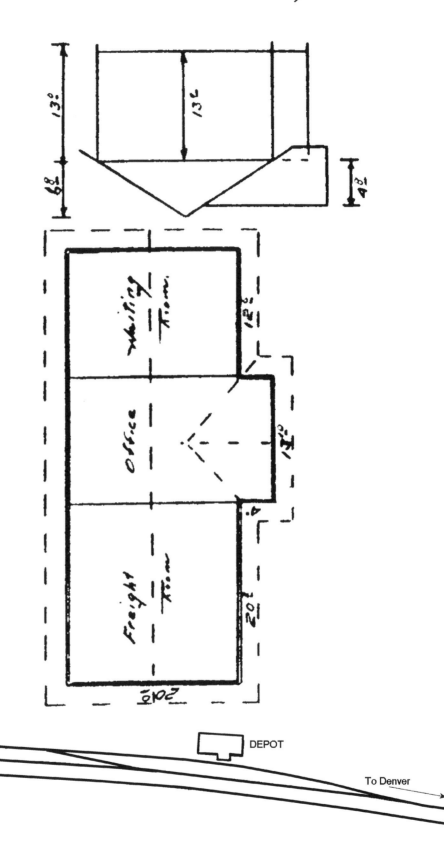

Lehi, UT

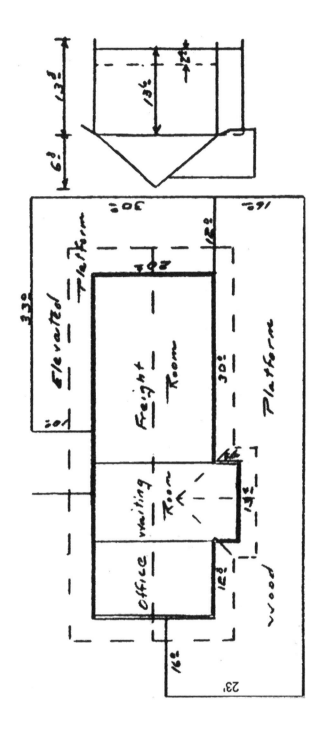

DEPOT

Built: 1895.
Construction: One-story frame structure of 20' x 56', with a 4' x 12' addition.
Roof: Gable, wood shingles.
Walls: Drop siding with 3'6" beaded wainscot.

Freight end converted to living quarters in 1943.
Retired 1949.

To Denver

Depot

ELEVATION: 4408'

DEPOT

Built: 1893.
Construction: One-story frame structure of 16' x 48', with additions of 18' x 23' and 5' x 12'.
Roof: Gable, wood shingles.
Walls: Drop siding with 4' beaded wainscot.

Retired 1950.

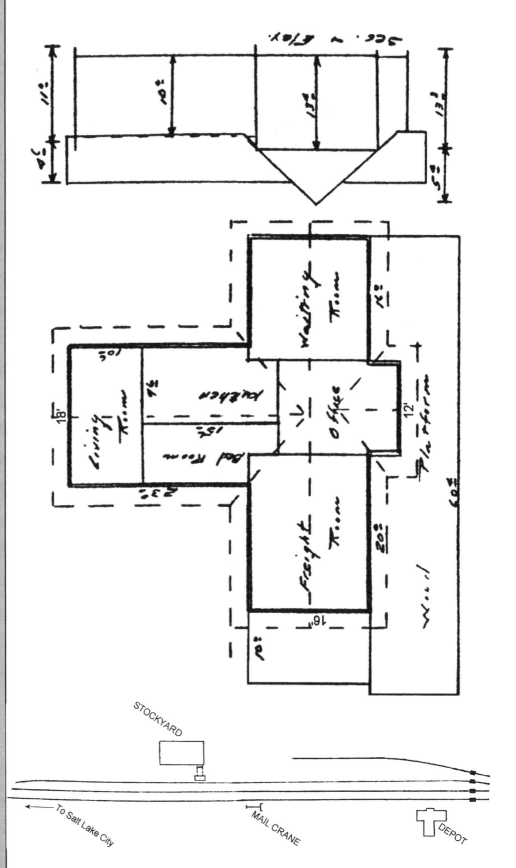

Murray Depot, UT

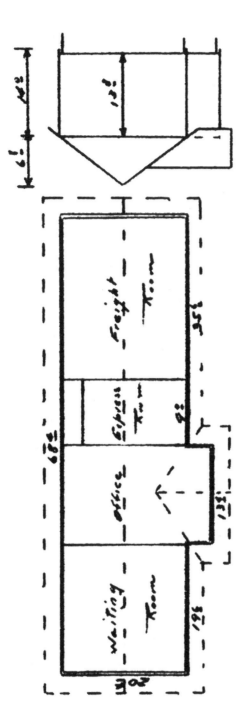

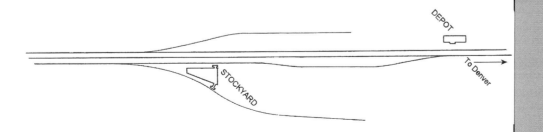

ELEVATION: 4289'

DEPOT

Built: 1896.
Construction: One-story frame structure of 20' x 68', with a 4' x 13' addition.
Roof: Gable, wood shingles.
Walls: Drop siding with a 3' beaded wainscot.

Location changed August 1915.

Retired 1953.

Salt Lake City, UT

ELEVATION: 4224'

FIRST PASSENGER DEPOT

Built: 1881.
Construction: Two-story frame structure of 32' x 75'.

Retired 1910

SECOND PASSENGER DEPOT

Built: 1910 (as Union Depot).
Construction: Two-story brick structure of 100' x 150' with a wing on both sides, each a one-story brick structure 70'x 130'.
As of writing, structure still exists.

FIRST FREIGHT DEPOT

Built: 1884.
Construction: One-story structure of 32' x 85'.
Frame and corrugated iron addition of 32' x 156' in 1909.

SECOND FREIGHT DEPOT

Built: 1918-9.
Outbound Freight House: Reinforced concrete, asbestos roof 56' x 400'.
Inbound Freight House: Reinforced concrete, asbestos roof 66' x 630'.

Woods Cross, UT

To Ogden →

Depot

FIRST DEPOT

Built: 1884.
Construction: One-story frame structure of 18' x 49', with a 4' x 15' addition.

Moved to Moroni 1915.

SECOND DEPOT

Built: Unlisted.
Construction: One story frame structure 16' x 20'.

Moved to Geneva 1942.

Kaysville, UT

DEPOT

Built: 1884
Construction: One and a half-story frame structure of 18' x 49', with 4' x 12' addition.
Roof: Gable, wood shingles.
Walls: Drop siding with 3'6" beaded wainscot.

Retired 1937.

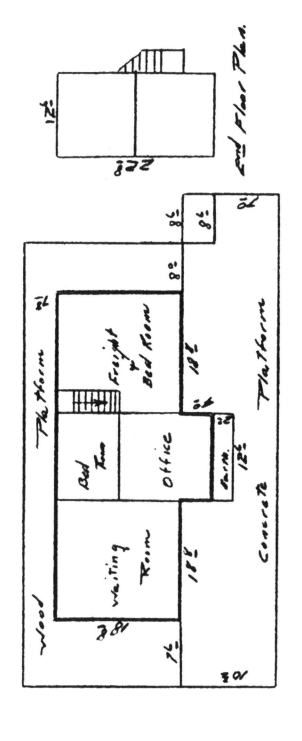

Layton, UT

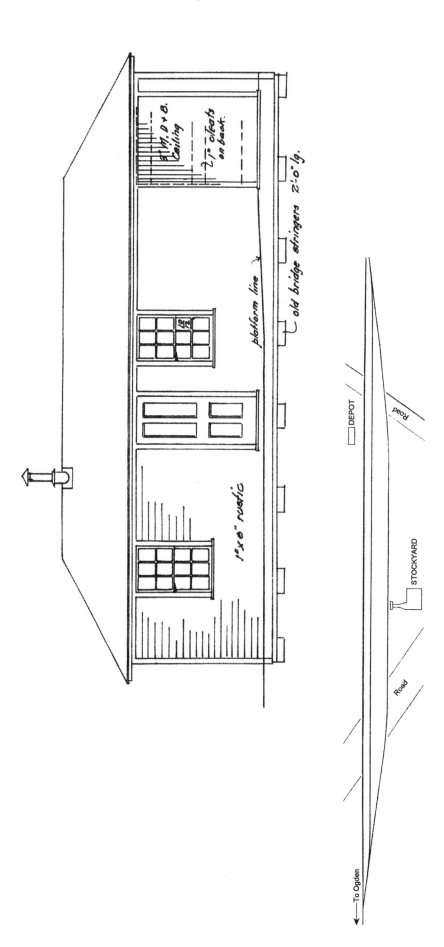

Dt.M. D + B.
Ceiling

2.7" cleats
on back.

platform line

old bridge stringers 2'-0" lg.

1" x 6" rustic

DEPOT

Road

STOCKYARD

Road

To Ogden

FIRST DEPOT

Built 1916.
Construction: One-story frame structure of 12' x 34'.
Roof: Hip, composition No.2.
Walls: Drop siding.

Retired 1949.

SECOND DEPOT

Built: 1949.
Construction: One-story cinder block structure of 24' x 36, with living quarters.
Walls: Cinder block

Retired 1970.

Clearfield, UT

ELEVATION: 4451'

DEPOT

Built: 1943.
Construction: One-story frame structure of 19' x 43'.

Retired after 1961.

To Salt Lake City →

DEPOT

Ogden, UT

DEPOT

Union depots owned by Union Pacific:
Built 1869 two-story frame structure.
Built: 1889. 3-story stone center, with a 2-story stone wing each side.
Rebuilt 1924 due to fire damage.

FIRST FREIGHT HOUSE

Built 1881-2.
Construction: Frame structure of 30' x 176'.

Destroyed by fire August 3, 1919.

SECOND FREIGHT HOUSE

Built: 1913-4.
Construction: Brick 56' x 40' and 45' x 194'.

Photos

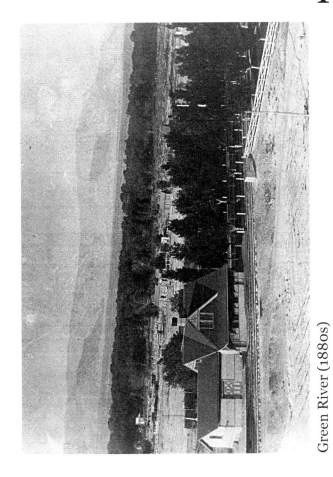

Green River (1880s)

Helper (1915)

Thompson

Price

Photos

Soldier Summit

Thistle (1948)

Colton

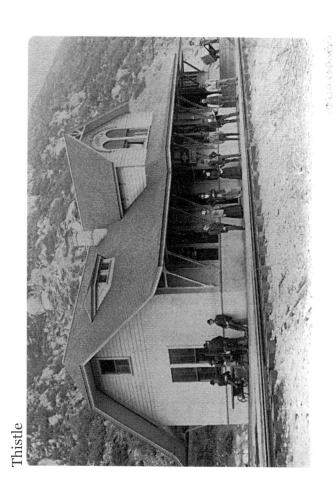

Thistle

Photos

Provo

Salt Lake City

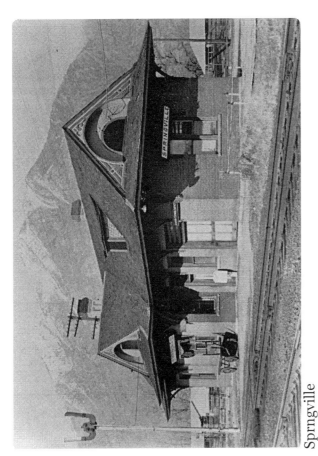

Sprngville

Riverton

88

UTAH BRANCH LINES

Miles from Denver to:

SUNNYSIDE BRANCH
Sunnyside, UT	620.4

PLEASANT VALLEY BRANCH
Scofield, UT	659.6

MARYSVALE BRANCH
Fairview, UT	713.2
Mount Pleasant, UT	719.8
Spring City, UT	725.2
Ephraim, UT	734.6
Manti, UT	742.0
Manti, UT- SPV RR	742.0
Gunnison, UT	750.7
Salina, UT	767.6
Sigurd, UT	777.4
Richfield, UT	784.9
Elsinore, UT	792.9
Sevier, UT	801.7
Marysvale, UT	813.4
Woods Cross, UT	753.6

SAN PETE VALLEY BRANCH
Moroni	745.9
Fountain Green	754.9

TINTIC BRANCH
Spanish Fork, UT	699.6
Payson, UT	706.6
Harold, UT	715.5
Goshen, UT	717.9
Knightville, UT	734.5
Eureka, UT	735.5
Silver City, UT	739.5

PROVO CANON BRANCH
Charleston, UT	722.7
Heber, UT	726.7

BINGHAM BRANCH
Midvale, UT	734.5
Bingham, UT	748.6

PARK CITY BRANCH
Sugar House, UT	745.3
Park City, UT	774.8

DEPOT

Built: 1900.
Construction: Two-story frame structure of 20' x 72', with a 4' x 13' addition.
Roof: Gable, wood shingles.
Walls: Drop siding, with 3' beaded wainscot.

Retired 1956.

Sunnyside, UT

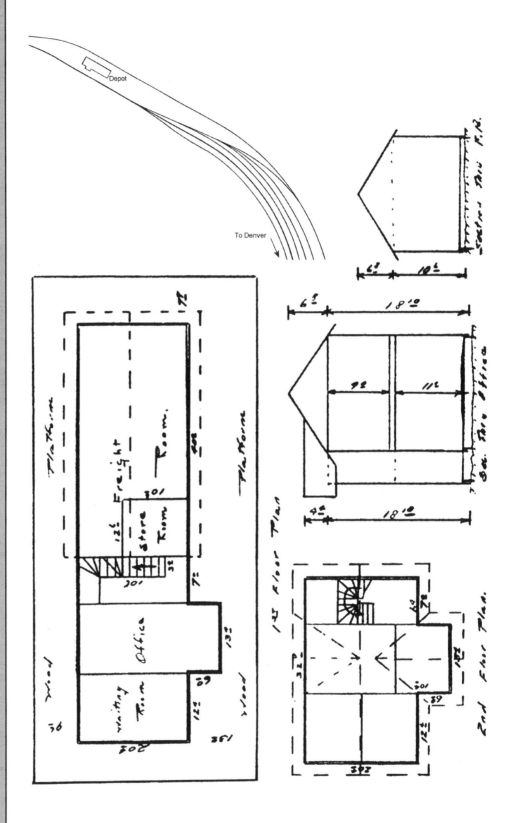

Scofield, CO

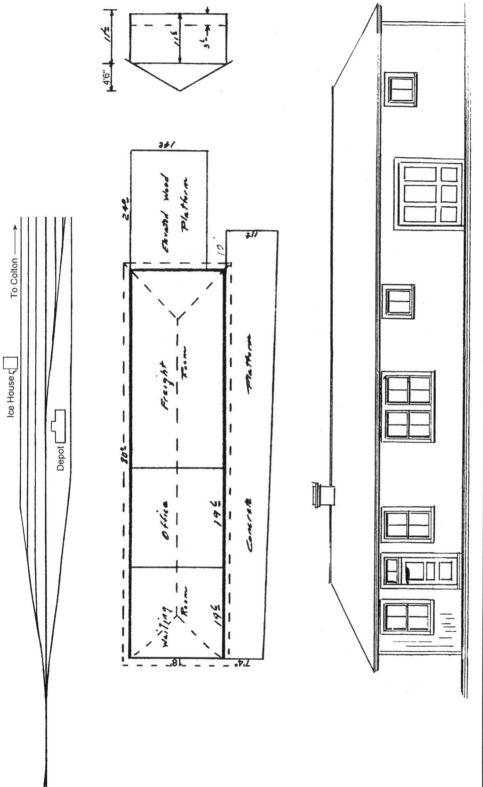

FIRST DEPOT

One-story frame structure construction of 18' x 57' with a 4' x 16' addition.
Destroyed by fire June 6, 1914.

SECOND DEPOT

Built: 1915.
Construction: One-story frame structure of 18' x 80'.
Roof: Hip, wood shingles.
Walls: board and batten.

Retired 1947.

Fairview, UT

ELEVATION 6033'

DEPOT

Built: 1890.
Construction: One-story frame structure of 16' x 40'.
Roof: Gable, wood shingles.
Walls: Board and batten.

Retired 1954.

To Denver

DEPOT

TANK

STOCKYARD

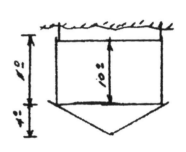

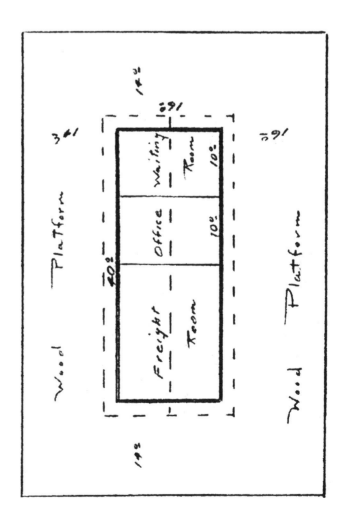

92

Mount Pleasant, UT 1-2

ELEVATION 5857'

<u>DEPOT</u>

Built: 1890.
Construction: One-story frame structure of 20' x 67', with a 3' x 16' addition.
Roof: Hip, wood shingles.
Walls: V-Joint, with 3'4" beaded wainscot.

Retired 1986.

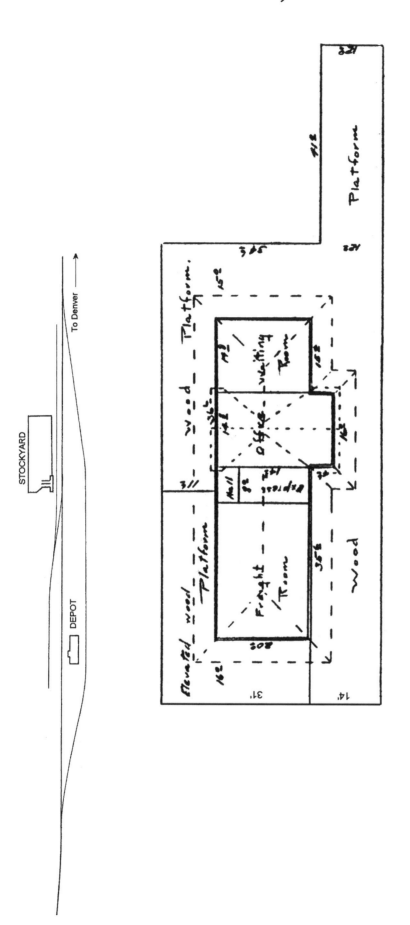

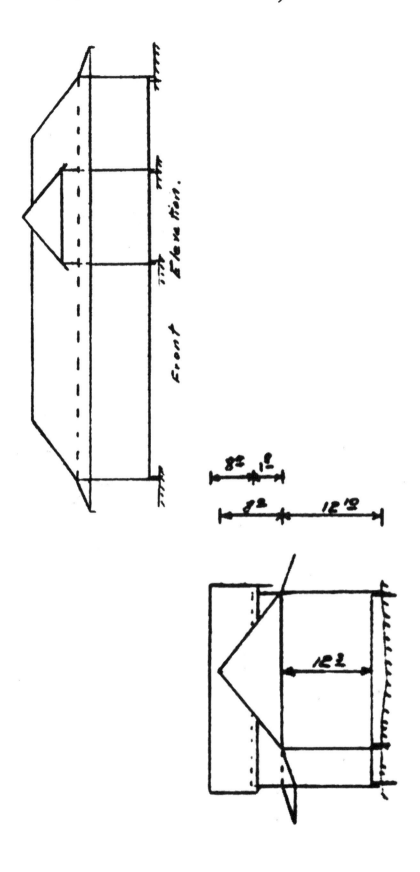

Spring City, UT

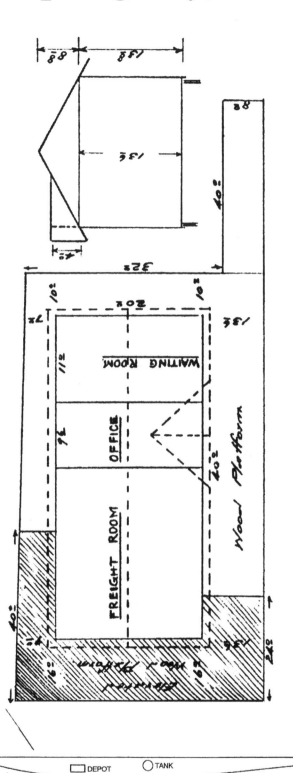

WAITING ROOM

OFFICE

FREIGHT ROOM

Wood Platform

To Denver →

County Rd.

☐ DEPOT   ○ TANK

STOCKYARD

ELEVATION 5696'

DEPOT

Built: 1893.
Construction: One-story frame structure of 20' x 40'.
Roof: Gable, wood shingles.
Walls: Drop siding with 3' beaded wainscot.

Retired 1947.

95

Ephraim, UT

DEPOT

Built: 1894.
Construction: One-story frame structure of 20' x 84', with a 4' x 12' addition.
Roof: Gable, wood shingles.
Walls and eaves: Wood shingles with 3'6" beaded wainscot.

Retired 1985.

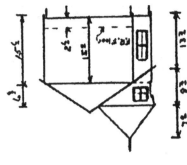

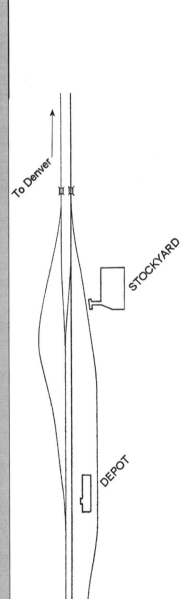

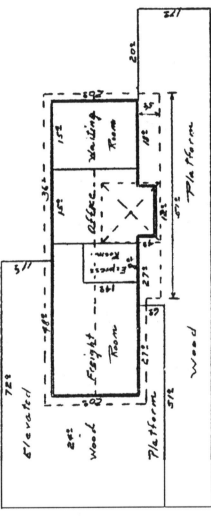

Manti, UT

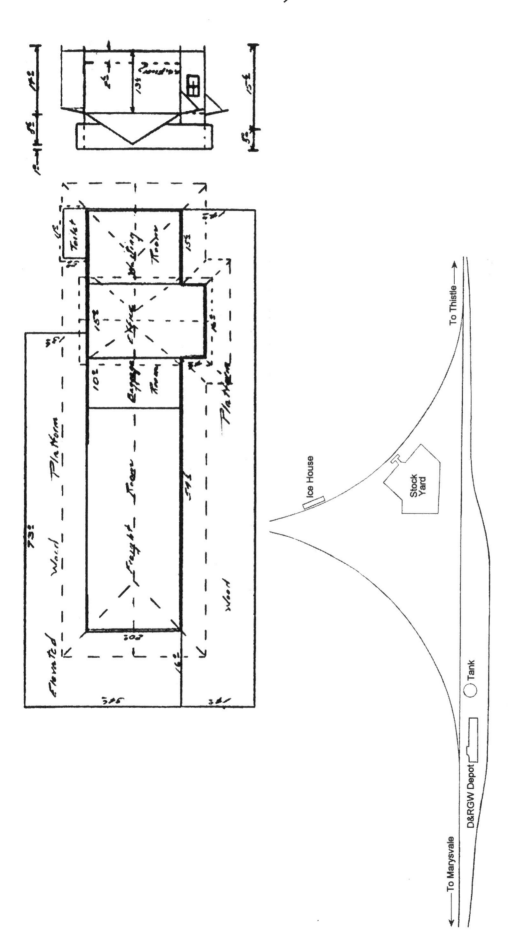

ELEVATION 5530'

DEPOT

Built: 1890.
Construction: One-story frame structure of 20' x 86', with 4' x 16' addition.
Roof: Hip, wood shingles.
Walls: Drop siding, with 3' 6" beaded wainscot.

Retired 1965.

To Thistle →

Ice House

Stock Yard

○ Tank

D&RGW Depot

← To Marysvale

97

ELEVATION 5540'

DEPOT

Built: 1893.
Construction: One- story frame structure of 20' x 45'.

Used as office building by 1920.
Retired 1930.

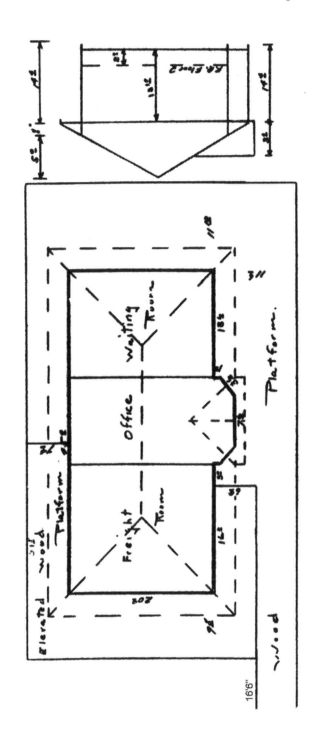

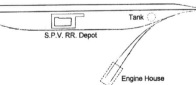

S.P.V. RR. Depot

Tank

Engine House

98

Gunnison, UT

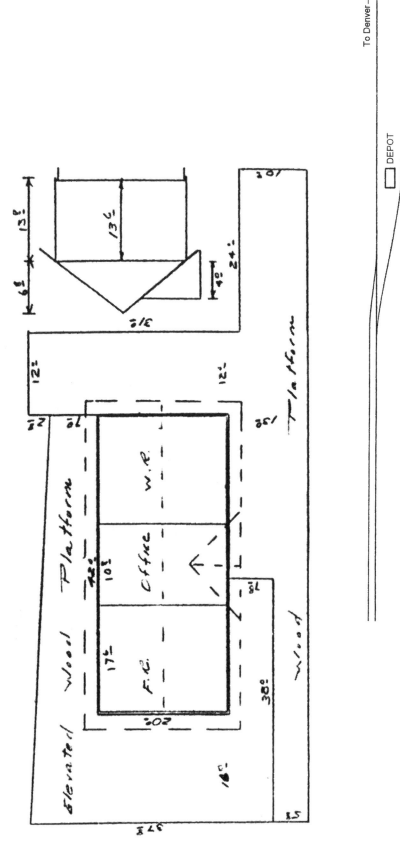

To Denver →

DEPOT

STOCKYARD

ELEVATION 5215'

DEPOT

Built: 1892.
Construction: One-story
frame structure of 20' x 42'.
Roof: Gable, wood shingles.
Walls: Drop siding with 3'
beaded wainscot.

Replaced 1935 by combining
depot with section foreman's
house.

Retired 1955.

Salina, UT

DEPOT

Built: 1893.
Construction: One-story frame structure of 20' x 59', with a 4' x 12' addition.
Roof: Gable, wood shingles.
Walls: Drop siding with a 3'2" beaded wainscot.

Extended to 65' by 1920.

Retired 1985.

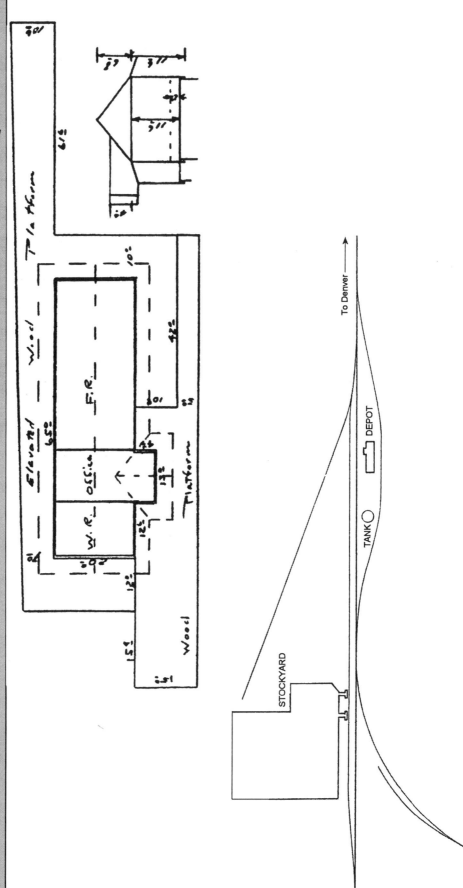

Sigurd, UT

FREIGHT ROOM
19'-6" x 37'-0"

EXPRESS

OFFICE
12'-0" x 24'-0"

WAITING ROOM
12'-0" x 19'-6"

PLATFORM 9'/33'

WAITING RM
12'·/21'·

OFFICE
12'·/24·

FREIGHT ROOM
21'·/36'·

DEPOT

STOCKYARD

To Denver →

DEPOT

Built: 1920.
Construction: One-story frame structure of 21' x 61', with a 3' x 12' addition.
A company preliminary drawing is shown.

Retired 1978.

Richfield, UT

ELEVATION 5308'

DEPOT

Built: 1896.
Construction: One-story frame structure of 20' x 72', with a 4' x 13' addition.
Roof: Gable, wood shingles.
Walls: Drop siding with a 4' beaded wainscot.

Toilets added 1917.

Retired 1985.

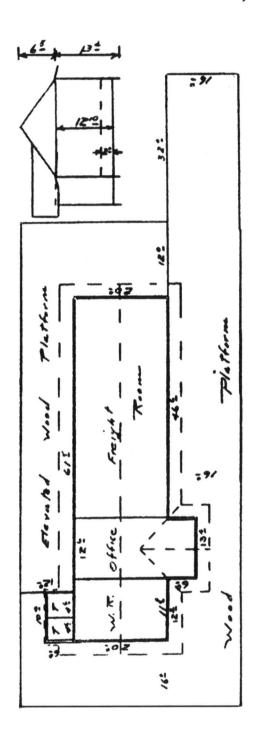

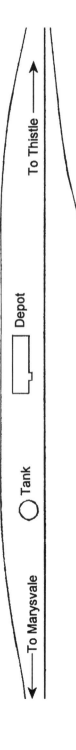

Elsinore, UT

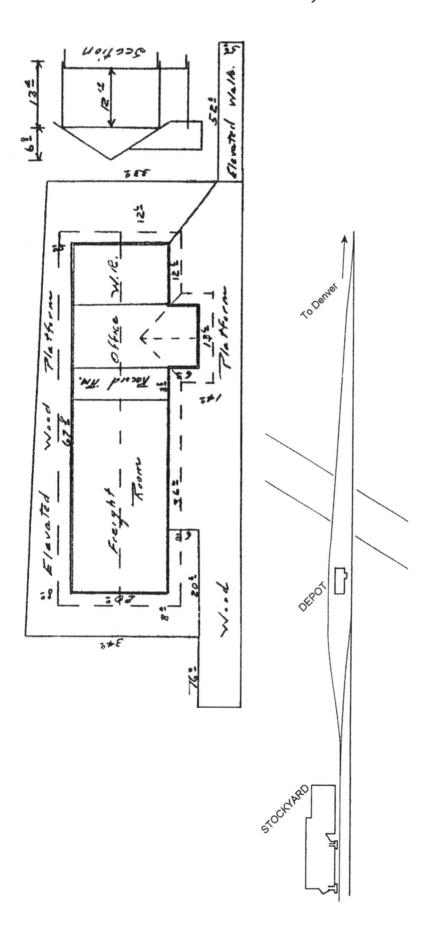

DEPOT

Built: 1896.
Construction: One-story frame structure of 20' x 67', with 6' x 13' addition.
Roof: Gable, wood shakes.
Walls: Drop siding with 4' beaded wainscot.

Retired 1953.

Sevier, UT

ELEVATION 5542'

FIRST DEPOT

Built: 1898.
One-story frame structure of
16' x 24'.

SECOND DEPOT

Built: 1900.
Construction: One-story
frame structure of 20' x 62'.
Roof – Gable, corrugated
iron.
Walls – Board and batten.

Converted to section house by
1920.

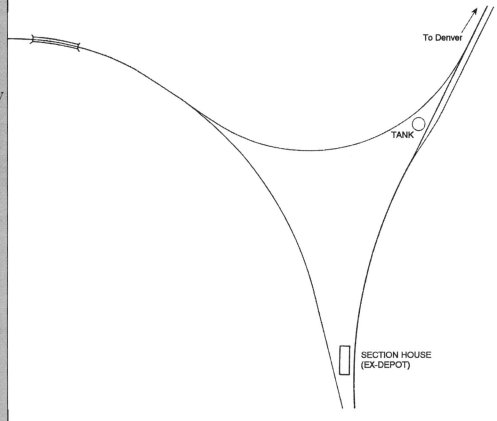

To Denver

TANK

SECTION HOUSE
(EX-DEPOT)

Marysvale, UT

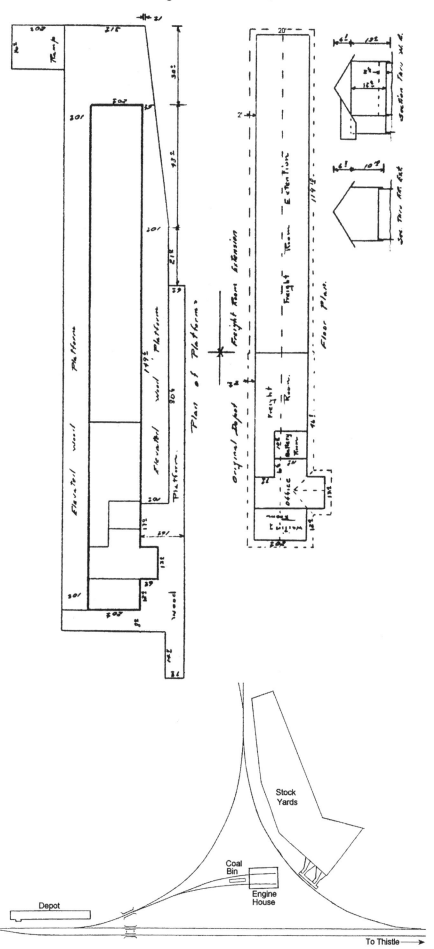

ELEVATION 5839'

DEPOT

Built: 1900.
Construction: One-story frame structure of 20' x 73', with a 6' x 13' addition. Freight room addition of 20' x 119' in 1909.
Roof – Gable, wood shingles.
Walls – Drop siding with 3' beaded wainscot; Freight room corrugated iron.

Retired partially in 1957 and completed in 1964.

Stock
Yards

Coal
Bin

Engine
House

Depot

To Thistle →

Moroni, UT

FIRST DEPOT

Built:
Construction: One-story frame 20' x 50'.

Demolished by 1915.
(No plans available)

SECOND DEPOT

Moved from Woods Cross in 1915.
Construction: One-story frame structure of 18' x 68', with a 4' x 12' addition.
Roof: Hip, wood shingles.
Walls: Drop siding with 3' beaded wainscot.

Retired 1976.

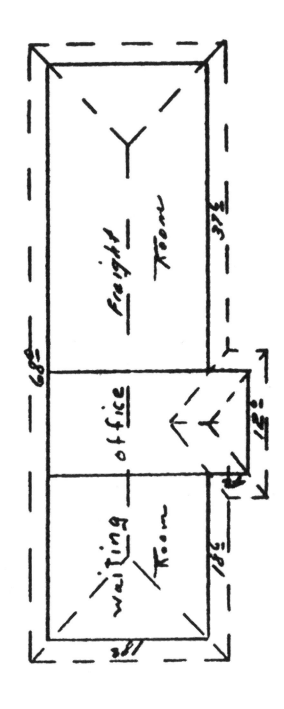

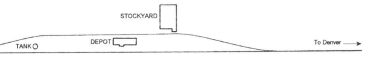

Fountain Green, UT

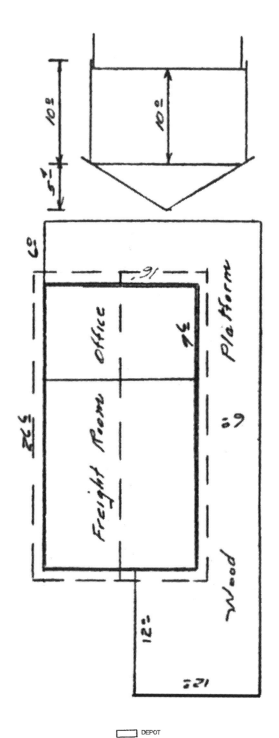

DEPOT

STOCKYARD

To Denver

ELEVATION 6000'

DEPOT

Built: by 1900.
Construction: One-story frame structure of 16' x 26'.
Roof: Gable, wood shingles.
Walls: Drop siding.

Freight room extended 20' in 1920.
Retired 1946.

Spanish Fork, UT

DEPOT

Built: 1894
Construction: One-story frame structure of 18' x 66' (ICC Valuation reported 18' x 58').
Roof: Gable, wood shingles.
Walls: Drop siding with 4' beaded wainscot.

Remodeled 1950.

Retired 1973.

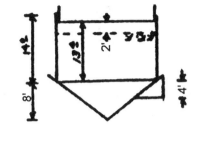

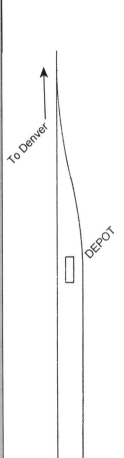

To Denver

DEPOT

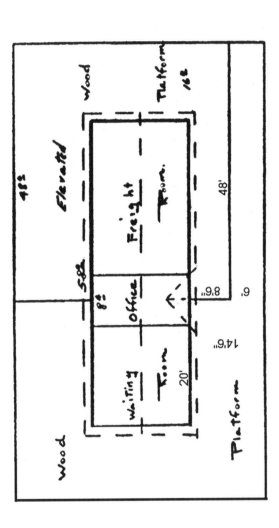

Payson, UT

Waiting Room

Office

Freight Room

202

58

88

88

72

Platform

Platform

Elevated 70'

Elevated 32'

Platform

Elevated 63'

18'

DEPOT

Built 1896.
Construction: One-story frame structure of 18' x 58' (similar to Spanish Fork).
Roof: Gable, wood shingles.
Walls: Drop siding with 4' beaded wainscot.

Retired 1961.

Harold, UT

DEPOT

Built: Reported 1891.
Construction: One-story frame structure of 16' x 24' and 26' x 48'.
Roof: Gable, composition 2 on lean to, wood shingles remainder.
Walls: Board and batten.

Retired 1955.

Goshen, UT

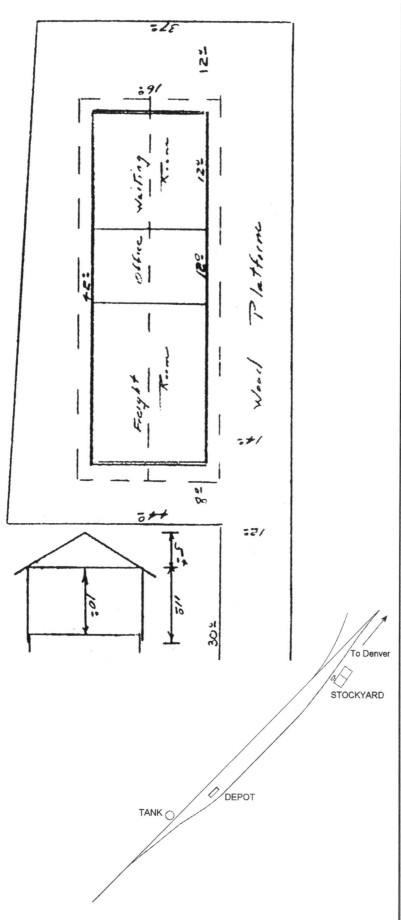

DEPOT

Built: 1891.
Construction: One-story frame structure of 16' x 42'.
Roof: Gable, corrugated iron.
Walls: Board and batten.

Retired 1947.

Knightville, UT

ELEVATION 6572'

DEPOT

Combination Waiting Room
and Tool House
Built: Not available
Construction: Structure of
corrugated iron 16' x 40'.
Walls: Corrugated iron
Roof: Gable
Retired by 1945.
(No drawing available.)

To Denver →

DEPOT

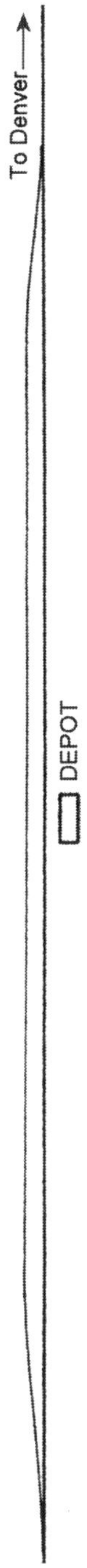

Eureka, UT

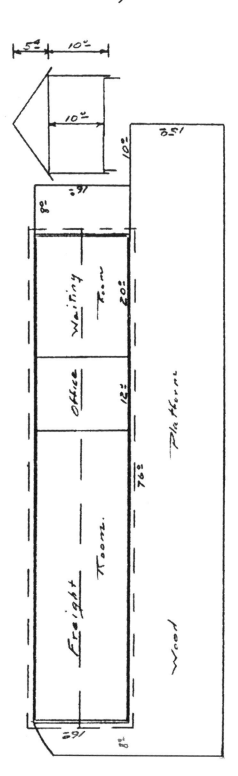

ELEVATION 6452'

DEPOT

Built: 1892.
Construction: One-story
frame structure of 16' x 76'.
Roof: Gable, corrugated iron.
Walls: Drop siding.

Retired 1964.
As of writing, depot still
exists.

ELEVATION 6100'

DEPOT

Built: 1892.
Construction: One-story
frame structure of 16' x 42'.
Roof: Gable, corrugated iron.
Walls: Board and batten.

Retired 1937.

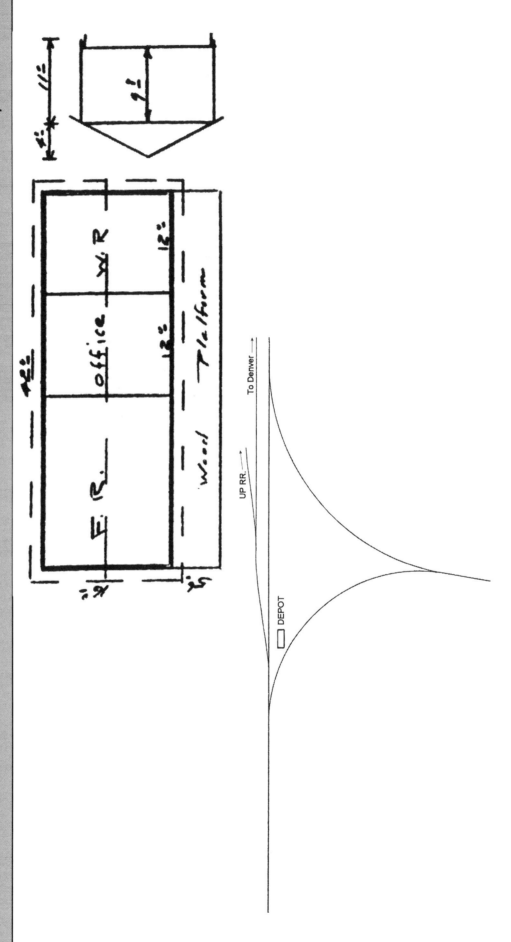

Charleston, UT

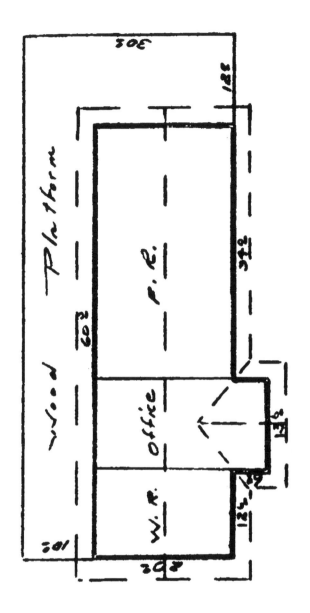

FIRST DEPOT

Built: 1899.
Construction: One-story frame structure of 20' x 60', with 6' x 13' addition.
Roof: Gable (peak height 20'), wood shingles.
Walls: Lap siding (height 12').

Retired c1940.

SECOND DEPOT

Built: 1942.
Construction: One-story frame structure of 16' x 24'.
Roof: Gable, with composition shingles.
Walls: Novelty siding.
(No plan available.)

Retired 1950.

To Denver →

☐ DEPOT

115

ELEVATION 5559'

DEPOT

Built: 1899.
Construction: One-story frame structure of 20' x 67', with a 6' x 13' addition.
Roof: Gable, wood shingles.
Walls: Drop siding with 3' beaded wainscot.

Retired 1971.
As of writing, this structure still exists.

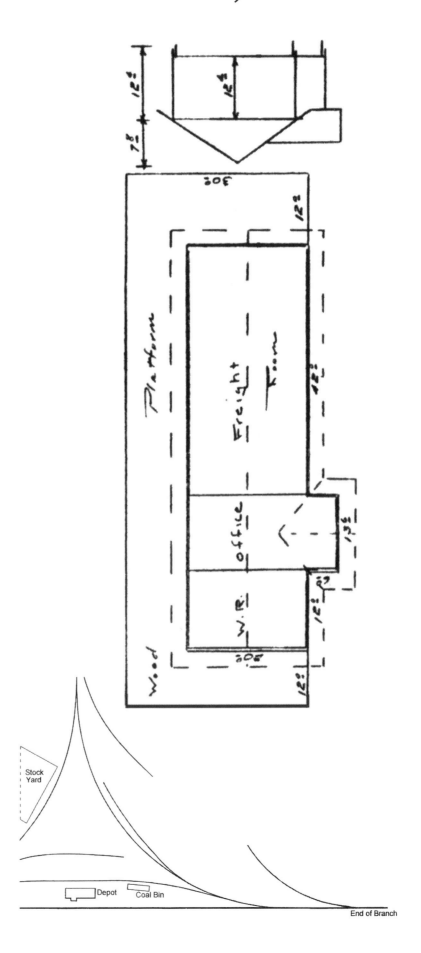

Midvale, UT

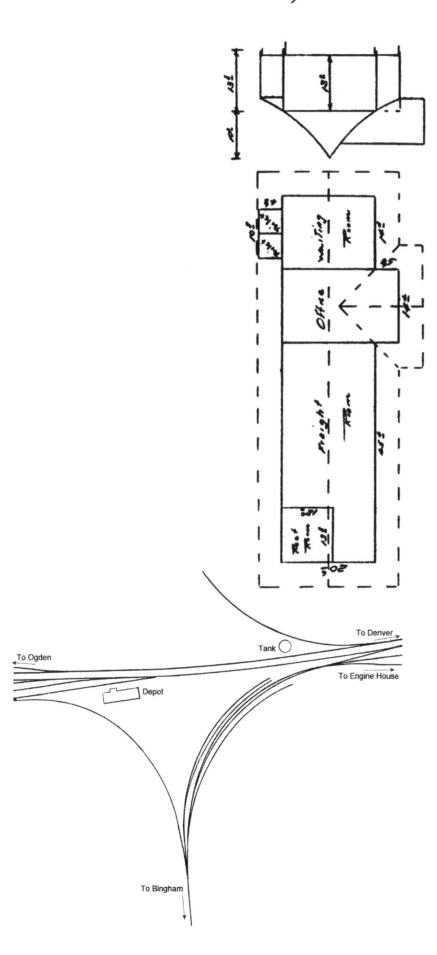

Tank

To Denver

To Ogden

To Engine House

Depot

To Bingham

DEPOT

Built 1894.
One-story frame structure of 20' x 74', with a 5' x 14' addition
Roof – Gable, wood shingles.
Walls – Drop siding, 3'6" beaded wainscot.

Toilets added 1917.
Reduced in size 1922.
Modernized 1948.

Retired 1969.

SECOND DEPOT
Built:1969.
One-story cinder block 20' x 40' x 8'
No depot plans available.

ELEVATION 5862'

DEPOT

Built: 1891.
Construction: One-story frame structure of 24' x 50' and 18' x 74' addition. 24' x 50' added to freight room 1904.
Roof: Gable, wood shingles.
Walls: Drop siding with a 3' beaded wainscot.

Retired 1954.

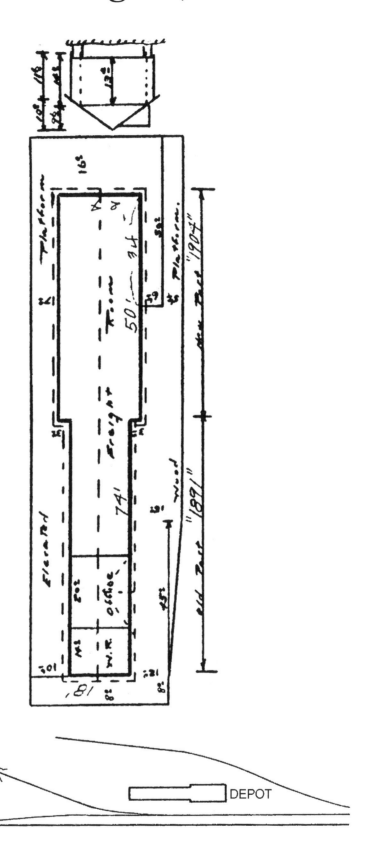

Sugarhouse, UT

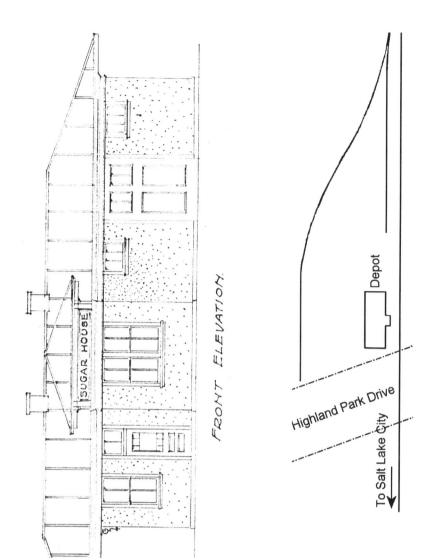

FRONT ELEVATION.

SUGAR HOUSE

Depot

Highland Park Drive

To Salt Lake City

DEPOT

Built 1917.
Construction: One-story
frame structure of 20' x 47'.
Roof: Hip, composition.
Walls: Stucco finish.
Freight room extended by 24'
1928.

Retired 1944.

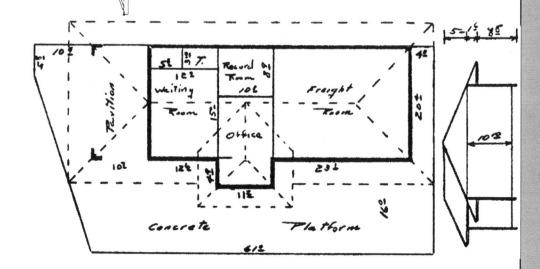

Waiting Room

Record Room

Office

Freight Room

Concrete Platform

Park City, UT

DEPOT

Built:1899.
Construction: One-story frame structure of 24' x 142'.
Roof: Gable, wood shingles.
Walls: Drop siding with 3' beaded wainscot.

Retired passenger section and 68' of freight room in 1947. Remaining 32' of freight room retired 1948.

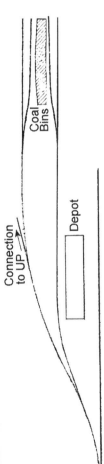

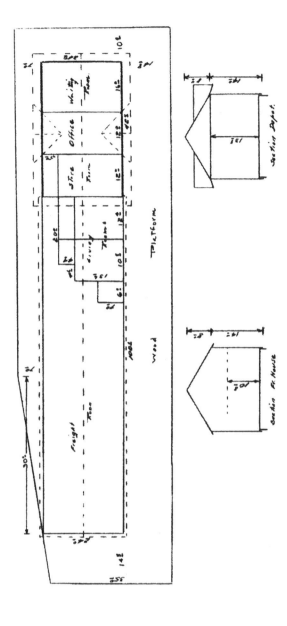

Photos

Ephraim (1910)

Gunnison

Scofield (1880's)

Manti

Photos

Heber

Park City

Payson (1914)

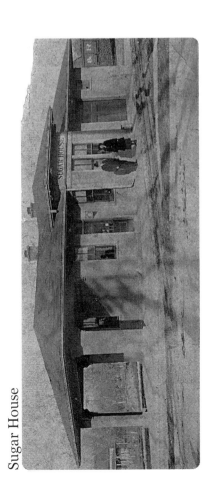

Sugar House

122

DENVER & SALT LAKE RAILWAY

Denver, CO	0	Granby, CO	76
Miramonte, CO	**	White Sulphur Springs, CO	86
Pine Cliff, CO	37	Kremmling, CO	103
Rollinsville, CO	42	McCoy, CO	134
Tolland, CO	47	Yampa, CO	162
Dixie Lake, CO	**	Phippsburg, CO	168
Arrow, CO	**	Oak Creek, CO	171
Irving, CO	**	Steamboat Springs, CO	191
Fraser, CO	62	Hayden, CO	215
Tabernash, CO	66	Craig, CO	231

Unless specified, miles are from Denver.
** Miles not shown in 1937 Official Guide.
Denver & Salt Lake Railway was acquired by the D&RGW in 1931.

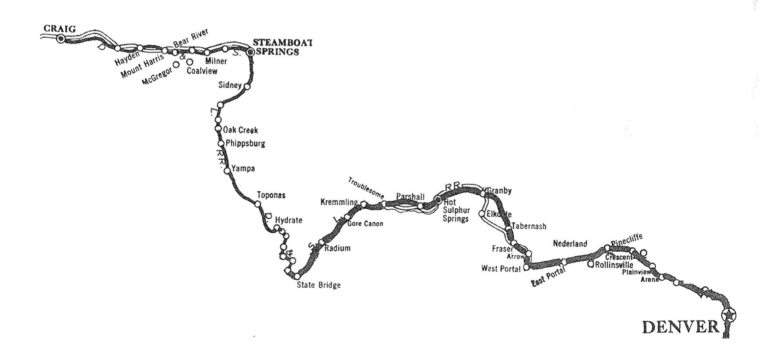

Denver (Moffat),CO

FIRST DEPOT

Built: 1904.
Construction: One-story brick structure of ~20' x 173'.

SECOND DEPOT

Built: 1906.
Construction: One and one-half story brick structure of 50' x 128'.
Walls: Brick

Retired: Unlisted.

Moffat Station

Miramonte, CO

DEPOT

Built: 1909.
Construction: One-story
frame structure of 12' x 24'.

Pine Cliff, CO

ELEVATION: Unlisted

<u>DEPOT</u>

Built: 1905.
Construction: One-story
frame structure of 14' x 36'.

Rollinsville, CO

OCT • 67 •

DEPOT

Built: 1913.
Construction: One-story brick structure of 24' x 55'.

Tolland, CO

DEPOT

Built: 1906.
Construction: One-story brick veneer structure of 16' x 60'.

Dixie Lake, CO

DEPOT

Built: 1913.
Construction: One-story
frame structure of 14' x 28'.

ELEVATION: Unlisted

DEPOT

Built: 1905.
Construction: One-story log structure of 23' x 65'.

Irvine, CO

DEPOT

Built: 1911.
Construction: One-story frame structure of 10' x 30'.

ELEVATION: Unlisted

DEPOT

Built: c.1920.
Construction: One-story frame structure.

Tabernash, CO

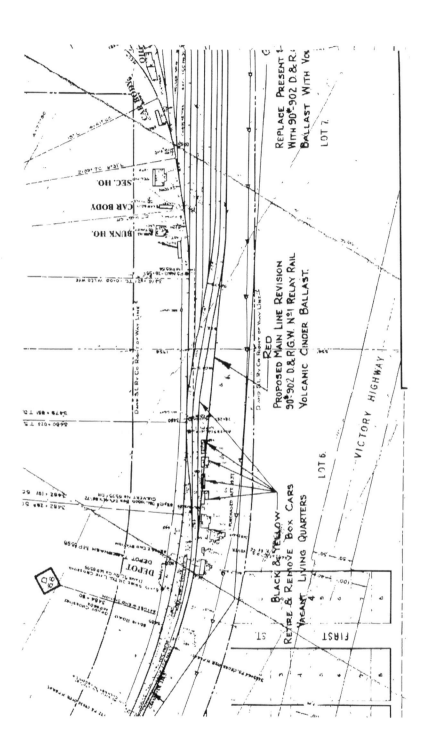

ELEVATION: Unlisted

DEPOT

Built: c.1920.
Construction: One-story frame structure 24' x irregular.

Granby, CO

DEPOT

Built: c.1906.
Construction: One-story
frame structure 24' x 80'.

Wasatch, CO

DEPOT

Built: c.1913.
Construction: One-story
frame structure 16' x 30'.

ELEVATION: Unlisted

DEPOT

Built: c.1906.
Construction: One-story
frame structure 24' x
irregular.

Kremmling, CO

DEPOT

Built: c.1906.
Construction: One-story
frame structure 24' x 80'.

McCoy, CO

ELEVATION: Unlisted

DEPOT

Built: c.1910.
Construction: One-story
frame brick 18' x 42'.

Yampa, CO

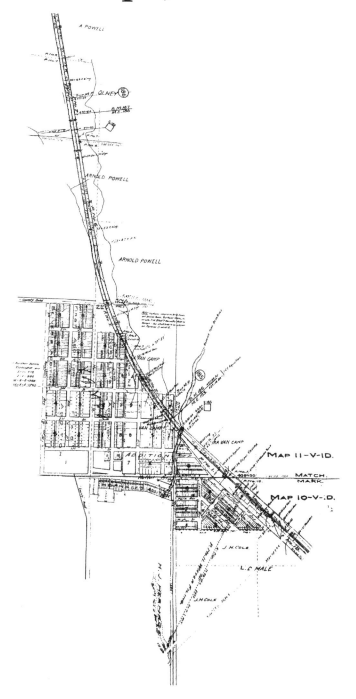

<u>DEPOT</u>

Built: c.1913.
Construction: One-story frame brick structure of 24' x 80'.

Phippsburg, CO

ELEVATION: Unlisted

DEPOT

Built: c.1911.
Construction: One-story
frame structure of 16' x 55'.

Phippsburg 1976

Oak Creek, CO

ELEVATION: Unlisted

DEPOT

Built: c.1913.
Construction: One-story frame structure brick.

Steamboat Springs, CO

DEPOT

Built: c.1909.
Construction: One-story brick structure of 26' x 80'.

1967

Hayden, CO

ELEVATION: Unlisted

<u>DEPOT</u>

Built: c.1918.
Construction: One-story brick structure of 26' x 79'.

1967

ELEVATION: Unlisted

DEPOT

Built: c.1917.
Construction: One-story brick structure of 26' x 80'.

1967

RIO GRAND SOUTHERN RAILROAD

Miles from Denver to:

Ridgway, CO	0
Placerville, CO	26.62
Vance Jct. CO	37.8
Ophir, CO	44.85
Rico,CO	66.24
Delores, CO	102.34
Mancos	123.5
Hesperus, CO	145.51
Telluride	82.9

Construction was 1890-1893.
RGS was an operating subsidiary of D&RG by June 1900.

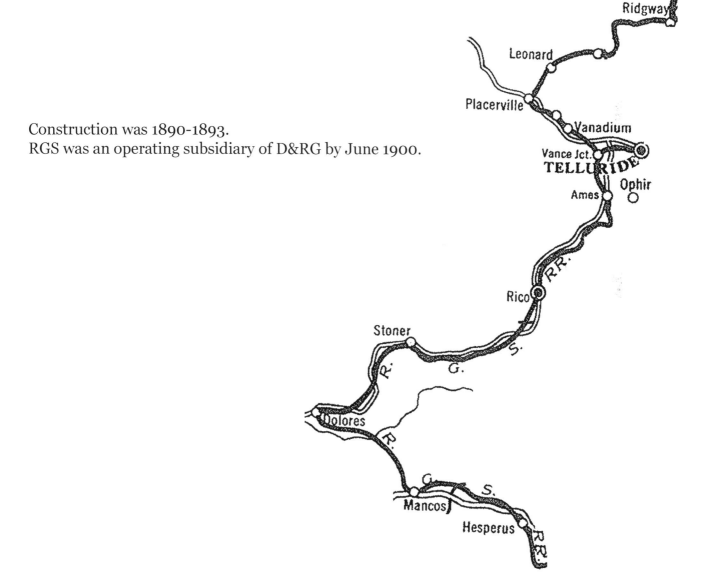

ELEVATION: 7003

DEPOT

Built: ~1890.
Construction: One-story frame structure of ~26' x 134'.

Fire in 1906, the facilities had to be re-built. The new facilities included a new five-stall roundhouse
The pride and joy of Ridgway was the new Queen Anne style depot that was constructed. The depot was a joint project of RGS and D&RG.

Placerville, CO

ELEVATION: Unlisted

DEPOT

Built: ~1890.
Construction: One-story
frame structure of 20' x 65'.

Vance Junction, CO

ELEVATION: Unlisted

DEPOT

Built: ~1890.
Construction: One-story
structure built from Ex-Pass.
Car No. 254.

Ophir, CO

ELEVATION: Unlisted

DEPOT

Built: ~1890.
Construction: One-story
frame structure of 20' x 90'.

Rico, CO

DEPOT

Built: Construction was 1890-1893.
Construction: One-story frame structure of 20' x 130'.

Delores, CO

ELEVATION: 6857'

DEPOT

Built: Construction was 1890-1893.
Construction: One-story frame structure of 20' x 80'.

FREIGHT DEPOT

Built: Construction was 1890-1893.
Construction: One-story frame structure of 24' x 96'.

Mancos, CO

DEPOT

Built: Construction was 1890-1893.
Construction: One-story frame structure of 20' x 90'.

Hesperus, CO

DEPOT

Built: Construction was 1890-1893.
Construction: One-story frame structure of 20' x 30'.

Retired: Destroyed by fire, May 4, 1940

ELEVATION: Unlisted

DEPOT

Built: Construction was 1890-1893.
Construction: One-story frame structure of 22' x 116'.

ACKNOWLEDGMENTS

The authors are grateful to the Colorado Railroad Museum, Golden, CO, and the assistance provided by Kenton Forrest and Sharon McGee, for the information presented in this book.

Additional information was obtained from the Interstate Commerce Commission records held by the National Archives, College Park, Maryland.

ALPHABETIC INDEX

Allison, CO	35	Gunnison, UT	99
Amargo, NM	29	Harold, UT	110
American Fork, UT	76	Hayden, CO	143
Antonito, CO	21	Heber, UT	116
Arboles, CO	34	Helper, UT	64
Arrow, CO	130	Hermosa, CO	42
Aztec, NM	46	Hesperus CO	153
Bingham, UT	118	Hot Sulphur Springs, CO	136
Castle Gate, UT	65	Ignacio, CO	36
Chama, NM	25	Irvine, CO	131
Charleston, UT	115	Juanita, CO	32
Cisco, UT	58	Kaysville, UT	82
Clearfield, UT	84	Knightville, UT	112
Colton, UT	67	Kremmling, CO	137
Craig, CO	144	Kyune, UT	66
Creede, CO	8	La Jara, CO	19
Cumbres, NM	24	La Madera (Mill), NM	50
Del Norte, CO	6	Layton, UT	83
Denver (Moffat), CO	124	Lehi, UT	77
Dixie Lake, CO	129	Loma, CO	54
Dolores, CO	151	Lumberton	30
Dulce, NM	31	Mack, CO	55
Durango, CO	37	Mancos CO	152
Elsinore, UT	103	Manti, UT	97
Embudo NM	14	Manti, UT- S.P.V. R.R.	98
Ephraim, UT	96	Mapleton, UT	72
Espanola NM	13	Marysvale, UT	105
Eureka, UT	113	McCoy, CO	138
Fairview, UT	92	Midvale, UT	118
Farmington, NM	48	Mill Fork, UT	70
Fountain Green	107	Miramonte, CO	125
Fraser, CO	132	Monero, NM	28
Fruita, CO	53	Monte Vista, CO	5
Geneva, UT	75	Moroni	106
Giluly, UT	69	Mounds, UT	62
Goshen, UT	111	Mount Pleasant, UT	93
Granby, CO	134	Murray Depot, UT	79
Green River, UT	60	Oak Creek, CO	141

ALPHABETIC INDEX

Ogden, UT	85
Ophir CO	149
Osier, CO	23
Pagosa Junction, CO	33
Pagosa Springs, CO	49
Park City, UT	120
Payson, UT	109
Phippsburg, CO	140
Pine Cliff, CO	126
Placerville Co	147
Price, UT	63
Provo, UT	74
Richfield, UT	102
Rico CO	150
Ridgway CO	146
Riverton, UT	78
Rockwood, CO	43
Rollinsville, CO	127
Romeo, CO	20
Ruby, CO	56
Salina, UT	100
Salt Lake City, UT	80
Santa Fe NM	15
Scofield, UT	91
Sevier, UT	104
Sigurd, UT	101
Silver City, UT	114
Silverton, CO	44
Soldier Summit, UT	68
Spanish Fork, UT	108
Spring City, UT	95
Springville, UT	73
Steamboat Springs, CO	142
Sublette, NM	22
Sugar House, UT	119
Sunnyside, UT	90
Tabernash, CO	133
Taos Junction NM	12
Telluride CO	154
Thistle, UT	71
Thompson, UT	59
Tolland, CO	128
Tres Piedras NM	11
Trimble, CO	41
Vance Jct. CO	148
Wagon Wheel Gap, CO	7
Wasatch, CO	135
Westwater, UT	57
Woods Cross, UT	81
Woodside, UT	61
Yampa, CO	139

PHOTOGRAPH INDEX

Allison, CO	39	Ogden, UT	85
Antonito, CO	26	Ophir CO	149
Arboles, CO	39	Osier, CO	38
Arrow, CO	130	Pagosa Junction, CO	33
Aztec, NM	51	Pagosa Springs, CO	49
Chama, NM	26	Park City, UT	122
Colton, UT	87	Payson, UT	122
Craig, CO	144	Phippsburg, CO	140
Creede, CO	9	Pine Cliff, CO	126
Cumbres, NM	26	Placerville Co	147
Del Norte, CO	9	Price, UT	86
Denver (Moffat), CO	126	Provo, UT	88
Dolores, CO	151	Rico CO	150
Dulce, NM	38	Ridgway CO	146
Durango, CO	39	Riverton, UT	88
Embudo NM	17	Rockwood, CO	93
Ephraim, UT	121	Rollinsville, CO	127
Espanola NM	17	Romeo, CO	26
Farmington, NM	51	Ruby, CO	56
Fraser, CO	132	Salt Lake City, UT	80, 88
Granby, CO	134	Scofield, UT	121
Green River, UT	86	Silverton, CO	45
Gunnison, UT	121	Soldier Summit, UT	87
Hayden, CO	143	Springville, UT	88
Heber, UT	122	Steamboat Springs, CO	142
Helper, UT	86	Sublette, NM	22
Hot Sulphur Springs, CO	136	Sugar House, UT	122
Ignacio, CO	39	Taos Junction NM	17
Kremmling, CO	137	Telluride CO	154
Lumberton	38	Thistle, UT	87
Mancos CO	152	Thompson, UT	86
Manti, UT	121	Tres Piedras NM	17
Monero, NM	38	Vance Jct. CO	148
Monte Vista, CO	5	Wagon Wheel Gap, CO	9
Oak Creek, CO	141	Yampa, CO	139

Made in the USA
Columbia, SC
25 November 2017